IF YOU ARE PRONE TO
worry, anger, anxiety, disconten̶t̶, f̶r̶u̶s̶-
tration and inadequacy, t̶h̶e̶ c̶o̶m̶m̶o̶n̶ i̶l̶l̶s̶ ̶o̶f̶
stress . . .

IF YOU ARE HAMS̶T̶R̶U̶N̶G̶
in your work, studies, cr̶e̶a̶t̶i̶v̶i̶t̶y̶, l̶o̶v̶e̶ a̶n̶d̶ other
personal relationships, a̶s̶ a̶ c̶o̶n̶s̶e̶q̶uence of stress . . .

IF YOU ARE THREATENED
by high blood pressure, heart attack, ulcers, insomnia, perhaps even cancer, to mention but a few
of the crippling and killing effects of stress . . .

IF YOU WANT TO LEARN
how you can change your harmful, erroneous beliefs
into more relaxing, realistic ones, and how meditation, progressive relaxation and self-hypnosis can
actually be used by any layperson to counter and
conquer stress . . .

STRESS, SANITY, AND SURVIVAL
is must reading for you!

ROBERT L. WOOLFOLK, Ph.D., assistant professor of
psychology at Rutgers University, is also a practicing psy-
chotherapist and trainer of clinicians. At present, he is involved in research on several stress-related topics.

FRANK C. RICHARDSON, Ph.D., associate professor of
educational psychology at the University of Texas at Aus-
tin, is also engaged in the part-time practice of psychotherapy. His recent research activities have focused on trying to
understand and assess the kind of anxiety that disrupts human performance in a number of everyday situations. Dr.
Richardson has also developed and evaluated several treatment programs for teaching people to cope more effectively with stress and anxiety.

stress,
sanity,
and survival

robert l. woolfolk
frank c. richardson

A SIGNET BOOK
NEW AMERICAN LIBRARY
TIMES MIRROR

contents

foreword

A number of books, magazines and newspaper articles have alerted us to the ravages of stress and have alarmed us about its seriousness. But few have offered concrete help in dealing with the problem. *Stress, Sanity, and Survival* not only offers the reader an improved understanding of stress, it also provides an effective program for coping with stress. It is rare to find a book that is both practical and theoretically sound, commonsensical and also clinically astute, profound, and yet plainspoken. *Stress, Sanity, and Survival* is such a book. It provides immediate answers for those of us who wish to cope more effectively with life in our complex and fast-changing society.

Drs. Woolfolk and Richardson present a great deal of useful information about stressful emotions and methods of coping with them. Part 1 blends the best insights from clinical and social psychology to give the reader a sound grasp of the stress problem. This section conveys an intimate "feel" for the everyday details of struggling with stress. Most readers will recognize themselves on these pages.

Many writings on the subject of stress tend to suggest that we are victims of stressful situations or victims of our emotional reactions to these situations. But Drs. Woolfolk and Richardson clearly show how we create the stress in our lives by thinking and behaving in ways that lead to worry, tension, and physical disease. Because we are often unaware of these patterns of thought and action, this section of the book can have a powerfully liberating effect on the reader.

Relatively few books have offered concrete help in dealing with the problems of stress. Some sources may suggest one or two useful techniques, such as meditation or relaxation training. But these methods are not presented in sufficient detail for readers to be able to apply them. In *Stress, Sanity, and Survival* the authors present easy-to-understand guidelines for coping effectively with stress. This is done with clarity and thoroughness. The book describes a comprehensive array of coping strategies that will show the reader how to deal with virtually all forms of stress.

Over the past twenty years, as an author and a trainer of psychotherapists, I have bent much of my effort counteracting the tendency to get "hung up" on just a few theories and techniques. There is no panacea for human suffering. Therapists need to be practical rather than dogmatic, diversified rather than narrow. We need to assemble many different kinds of effective treatments and apply them systematically to the problems of living that we all face. This outstanding book offers the wisdom and benefits of such a broad-based program to everyone concerned with stress.

I have recommended to many of my patients, students, and friends that they read this book and keep it around for ready reference. *Stress, Sanity, and Survival* goes as far as a book can in putting the psychologist's insights, skills, and tools in the hands of the layperson. But in addition to a remarkable distillation of what psychology has to say about stress, there is in this book a philosophical depth that is exceptional in writings of this kind. Life is not oversimplified but is portrayed in its proper complexity. As a result, the reader is afforded the rare opportunity to learn how better to cope with stress, as well as the rarer opportunity to gain some measure of wisdom.

Arnold A. Lazarus, Ph.D.
Professor
Graduate School of Applied & Professional Psychology
Rutgers University

acknowledgments

In the writing of this book it has been apparent to us throughout that we owe many debts to the work of others. If we have managed a clear view of the landscape of stress, it is largely because we have stood on the shoulders of giants who have gone before us. We have built upon the basic theoretical and empirical work of Alfred Adler, Albert Ellis, Arnold Lazarus, Richard Lazarus, Morton Deutsch, and Donald Meichenbaum. We have profited greatly from discussions with Paul Lehrer, Ollie Bown, Patricia Carrington, Guy Manaster, and Bert Brown. We are grateful to Mary Yost for her support and encouragement. Mary Teague and Anita Woolfolk deserve special thanks both for their invaluable critical advice and their almost indefatigable abilities to accept and cope with this project. Finally, we would like to thank the many other friends, students, and clients who read and reacted to portions of the manuscript.

R.L.W.
F.C.R.

stress, sanity, and survival

part 1

the nature
of stress

1

introduction

The stress of life is inescapable. No matter what we do we cannot entirely avoid it. When society was less complex and life slower paced, it was unnecessary for most citizens to set out to avoid stress. The stress of earlier times was not a serious threat to health and happiness.

But times have changed. The technological developments of the last fifty years have created a world in which stress is a danger to each of us. The alarming statistics show not only a rise in the level of psychological tension and anxiety, but also a dramatic increase in the incidence of such stress-related diseases as hypertension and coronary disease. These diseases were relatively uncommon only half a century ago.

Many of us have come to live with, accept, and adapt to stress in such a way that we are no longer even aware of its effect on our health and sense of well-being. A moderate level of stress can become such a regular part of a person's life that it may be taken for granted as inevitable or, after years of adaptation, not even noticed. And although a person may not be acutely bothered by the stress in his life, he may still

3

be in danger. Chronic stress can cause ulcers, hypertension, coronary disease, many allergies, migraine and tension headaches, and numerous other physical maladies.

Even those who are painfully aware of the stress in their lives often do not know how to cope with it. They are pretty much in the position of the man who is told by his family doctor that he must learn to relax, knows that he needs to, but does not know how.

Our program of stress reduction is grounded solidly in scientific research. We have chosen to present methods which are both effective and relatively easy to learn. In subsequent chapters we will present the reader with tools for drastically reducing stress. But before we begin the attack on stress, we must come to know our adversary well.

A Model of Stress

A meaningful analysis of any phenomenon requires that it be clearly defined. Previous writings geared to popular audiences have provided a useful service by informing the public about the danger of stress, but they have not produced a definition of stress which aids the average individual in his attempts to deal with it. In the next few pages we will present a comprehensive and easily understandable model of stress. It will form the basis of an understanding of how stress operates to produce its debilitating effects. The model will provide the framework within which we will present methods for effectively coping with stress.

Some of our problems in fashioning a specific and useful definition of stress stem from the concept of stress itself. The term *stress* in psychology and medicine was borrowed from physics and engineering, where it meant something quite precise, namely the application of sufficient force to an object or system to distort or deform it. Perhaps this original meaning of the word has kept us thinking too long in terms of forces outside ourselves in the environment that, if strong enough, inevitably or automatically produce "strain," tension, or disease. Thus we tend to think of ourselves as carried along by social forces or trends quite beyond our control.

In his recent book *The Relaxation Response*, Herbert Benson defined stress as "environmental demands that require *behavioral adjustment*." It can be seen that here, as in physics,

4

stress is defined as some set of objective conditions in the environment that require a response from the person. Hans Selye, the eminent physician who conducted much of the early research on the physiological effects of stress, has defined stress in terms of the physiological response of the body to any demand made upon it.

The problem with both of these definitions is that they clearly conceptualize stress as something that affects people in an automatic, reflexlike way. They imply a model of human functioning which does not take into account the congnitive-appraisal system (the parts of our brains that perceive and evaluate the environment). The work of R. S. Lazarus has clearly pointed to the limitations of these mechanistic conceptions of stress. It is our contention that events do not in themselves produce stress reactions. Events in and of themselves are neutral. We hold that it is primarily our perceptions or appraisals of events that make them stressful. For example, if an employer criticizes an employee for poor performance on a work project, the amount of stress is almost exclusively a function of the employee's understanding of the significance of the reprimand. If the employee is married to the boss's sister and has air-tight job security, he will likely respond to the reprimand with less emotional arousal than if he is already in disfavor, has no such security blanket, and sees the boss's displeasure with him as a likely prelude to the unemployment line.

Environments place demands or requirements only to the extent that the demands are perceived or experienced. A daughter whose father desperately wants her to choose marriage over a career will not experience stress if her father never communicates the preference in any fashion. Even if the demand that she marry is made explicitly, the daughter may react with little stress if she believes she can persuade her father to change his mind, or if she has learned to disregard her father's statements in this area. Environmental demands are reacted to as demands only if they are understood and taken seriously.

Demands can also fail to produce stress if they are seen as unimportant or implying no consequences. A husband learns not to be influenced by his wife's demands for a new house if his experiece with her has taught him that he can ignore her "requirements" with impunity. However, if her demand is represented as a do-this-or-else issue supported by evidence of having consulted a divorce attorney, then the situation is entirely different with respect to its stress-arousing potential.

We would also contend that demands not only must be both perceived and consequential to produce stress, they must also call into question the degree to which the individual believes he can respond with success and comfort. Most of us believe that regular oil changes in our automobiles are desirable and necessary. The prospect of finding an hour to accomplish this on a leisurely Saturday afternoon would induce little emotional arousal. However, as the authors' own experience would confirm, it can be quite another matter when time must be found on an overcrowded Saturday schedule filled with professional, marital, parental, and clinical duties. Capability to respond to the perceived demand is crucial. A brilliant mathematics student suffers little anxiety when faced with the necessity of making an above-average score on a college-entrance test of mathematical ability. Not so the student who has consistently failed high school mathematics courses. Thus, for a stress reaction to occur the individual must perceive a demand which is of import and which calls into question his or her ability to cope successfully and painlessly. These then, are the conditions necessary to produce a stress reaction. Stress as we define it is not "out there" in the environment. It is "in here" within the human brain. It occurs between the stimulus and the response. Stress is always linked to some act of understanding resulting from the interaction between the environment and the organism.

To complete our model of stress we must describe the reaction of the organism to stress, and, in so doing, complete our definition of stress. Research has shown us that stress arouses, alerts, or otherwise activates the organism. This arousal or activation may be intellectual, behavioral, emotional, or physiological. A student undergoing the stress of an exam may achieve levels of intellectual alertness which surpass that of his or her normal functioning. A soldier on guard duty in wartime will move quickly to respond to evidence of potentially hostile activity. It is readily apparent that perceptions of negative consequences result in emotional upheavals. Similarly, some degree of physiological activation accompanies all stress. The arousal that is most often linked to stress is that of the fight-or-flight response. An understanding of this response requires a brief digression on that marvel that required millions of years of evolution to produce—human physiology.

Most products of that physiological evolution continue to serve us well. Our associative cortex is a data-processing miracle more complicated than any manmade computer. Our respiratory, circulatory, and digestive systems continue to adapt well to the demands of modern life. In general, we are quite fortunate that though the world has turned many times since the prehistoric era, most features of the human organism remain relatively well adapted to contemporary life. Most features, but not all.

One product of human evolution which each of us is born with is what the famous American physiologist Walter Cannon labelled the fight-or-flight response. This is a coordinated pattern of responses that occurs whenever the body responds to a perceived "emergency." When primitive man was confronted with such dangers from intruding predators, his automatic nervous system prepared him to respond to the threat either by speedy retreat or aggressive attack. Sights or sounds which might indicate danger activated the fight-or-flight response and produced a patterned, reliable series of changes.

The sound of an approaching animal would arouse the sympathetic branch of the autonomic nervous system. The part of the brain stem known as the hypothalamus would activate the pituitary gland, causing it to release the hormone ACTH into the bloodstream. This hormone travels in the blood to the adrenal glands, which are situated above the kidneys. The adrenals then secrete various steroids (among them adrenalin and cortisone) into the blood. These hormones circulate through the body causing changes that are important to any organism that must attack or flee in order to survive. Blood is diverted from our internal organs to our brains and skeletal muscles, providing us with energy for quick thinking and vigorous physical activity. The pupils of our eyes dilate, making them more sensitive to gradations in light. Hearing becomes more acute. Our hands and feet perspire. Our blood pressure is elevated. Our heart rate increases. Our breathing becomes more rapid, and our oxygen consumption increases. These reactions occur automatically once a situation is perceived as threatening. Accompanying these physiological changes very often are the emotions we associate with fighting or fleeing—anger or fear, respectively.

Once we believe ourselves to be threatened by future discomfort, our physiology and emotions respond relatively automatically. The fact that arousal is the automatic result of stress should not lead us to believe that the fight-or-flight response is a direct response to changes in the environment. The environment impinges upon us only through the filter of our perception and understanding. The construction we place upon events determines the degree of stress and hence the emotional and physiological response.

Our definition of stress is now complete: Stress is a perception of threat or expectation of future discomfort that arouses, alerts, or otherwise activates the organism.

Our model of stress suggests that there are three levels or components of the stress reaction: the environment, the appraisal and evaluation of the environment, and the reaction of emotional and physiological arousal. Events in the environment give rise to stress. Our belief that negative consequences will follow from events actually causes stress. Emotional and physiological arousal follow stress in a relatively automatic way once this negative appraisal is made. Reducing stress means the elimination of the debilitating physical and emotional changes that occur during the last phase of the stress reaction. Our model of stress indicates that, in principle at least, this last phase could be prevented at any of three levels.

As a first step, we could alter the environment so as to prevent the occurrence of events that are likely to produce stress. For example, we might change jobs or move to another part of the country. Often people yearn to simplify their lives and slow down their pace of living. But most people don't know how to do this without making radical changes that would result in giving up as much as would be gained. Most of us have freedoms, opportunities, and aspirations that are important to us and that are inextricably bound up in our current life styles. Our fantasies of escaping from the rat race are usually not realistic and do not provide a very practical guide to action. Subsequent chapters, "Managing Your Life Style" and "Resolving Interpersonal Conflicts," will attempt to demonstrate to the reader exactly how life-enhancing changes

8

can be made without disrupting those institutions and relationships that one values.

From our model it is also clear that a second front in the battle against stress could be the emotional and physiological response to stress. The connection between the fight-or-flight response is, as we have mentioned previously, an automatic one. Stress elicits this response of emotional and bodily arousal much in the manner of a reflex. However, the connection between stress and arousal can be weakened so that even perceptions of the most dire situations will not produce arousal. One method of accomplishing this is to lessen the body's capacity to be aroused by the ingestion of tranquilizing medication. Most drugs that have a depressant action on the central nervous system (such as alcohol, morphine, and barbiturates) will, if taken in sufficient quantities, lower the capacity of the individual to be aroused. The group of drugs known as tranquilizers (Valium, Librium, Miltown) is used almost exclusively for this purpose. The problems with the use of chemical methods to lower arousal are too complex and numerous to be discussed here. Suffice it to say that although these chemicals have many legitimate uses, they also possess many undesirable side effects and are frequently subject to abuse. Fortunately, there are several techniques for producing lowered arousal without the aid of drugs. We will describe three such methods in our chapters "Meditation," "Self-Hypnosis and Autosuggestion," and "Progressive Relaxation."

The third manner in which stress could be prevented is through altering those beliefs, assumptions, and ineffective ways of thinking that make us more vulnerable to stress. The idea of altering one's emotional response to the world by changing the way one thinks is as old as the Stoic philosopher Epictetus and as recent as the psychologist Albert Ellis. Since our perceptions and evaluations of the world actually cause stress, then changing some part of our basic outlook on life may be the most expedient way to reduce tension and anxiety. Changing one's attitudes can be a difficult undertaking, but often less difficult than modifying the basic circumstances of one's life. Altering our environment may create as much stress as it eliminates. Internalized philosophical changes, on the other hand, are with us always, helping us to cope with any situation we encounter. This third approach is worth elaborating because it is often misunderstood.

In much popular writing the connections between thinking, stress, and emotion are seen as reflecting a battle of mind versus body, logic versus feeling, rational thinking versus irrational emotions. The mind knows that stressful events do not warrant emergency emotional reactions. It is also capable of figuring out better ways of coping with stressful situations. But the body and its emotional reactions that are triggered by stress nevertheless continue to overreact to these situations. Unpleasant and disruptive emotions either cloud our thoughts and turn them toward the irrational, or they keep on occuring in spite of efforts to think and cope rationally. Thus we say to ourselves things like "I know I shouldn't get so angry about such a little thing like that, but I just can't control my emotions," or "I know it doesn't make any sense to feel so anxious, but no matter how hard I try to think rationally about it my emotions just take over and I panic," or "I know I need to relax and take things less seriously, but by the end of the day I'm feeling just as tense and driven as ever." The trouble, however, is that this kind of exercise of reasoning and willpower seldom works. We "try to relax," but in so doing strain and exert effort that produces additional physical tension and emotional arousal. Then we may add fuel to the flames by criticizing or punishing ourselves for not being able to relax better! That, in a nutshell, is what comes of the battle between reason and emotions; or rather, that is what comes of viewing the problem of coping with stress as this kind of battle.

One of the purposes of this book is to redirect the reader's attention back to the sphere of thinking and evaluating, back to the psychological domain that is usually the source of problems with stress. It is usually what we are thinking, or how we are thinking, or both, that creates stressful situations. Our thought processes actively create the chronic feelings of anger, anxiety, and frustration that plague both body and mind. Our thoughts and evaluations about ourselves and stressful situations are frequently to some degree mistaken. Often they are riddled with misconceptions and contradictions that have a profound effect on how we behave and feel in critical life situations. A cardinal principle (perhaps *the* cardinal principle) of human functioning is that it is not events in themselves but how we view them that causes emotional distress. Our thoughts may involve mistaken or contradictory beliefs about ourselves and the situations we face, or irrational, negative evaluations of ourselves and others, that make emotional distress inevitable.

Looking at things from this perspective we can arrange for an immediate armistice, if not a final peace treaty, in the war between reason and emotion. Generally speaking, thoughts and feelings simply do not conflict with each other. Feelings tend to follow thoughts. They go together. Feelings are by-products of the way we perceive, evaluate, and think about situations in living. Perceiving a situation to be dangerous to one's self-esteem or practical interests tends to make one anxious and panicky. On the other hand, believing you will succeed in some endeavor may produce feelings of pleasant anticipation. Beliefs, thinking, problem solving, behavior, and feelings are different, coordinated aspects of the whole person as he or she moves toward chosen goals. Inner division and conflict usually come not when there is a clash between reason and emotion, but when there is a clash among contradictory goals or directions in living. It is not a war of thoughts and feelings, but of thoughts with thoughts, beliefs with beliefs.

The clash of goal with goal or belief with belief often takes the form of wanting to have our cake and eat it too. Thus many of us in the United States want to, and believe we can, reach both the goal of being highly successful in nearly all aspects of our lives and the goal of being liked by nearly everyone we come in contact with. Each of these goals is highly unrealistic and stress-producing in and of itself. In addition, the goals are incompatible. You cannot compete with other people, be more successful than they are, and have everybody like you at the same time. If you simultaneously pursue these mutually exclusive goals, you inevitably will experience some of the symptoms of stress: frustration, tension, anxiety, and hostility.

We are often unaware of the contradictory or unrealistic nature of our outlook or thinking. Partly that may be because it is more pleasant for an individual to view him- or herself as having good intentions that are interfered with by troublesome emotions than to admit that those emotions may be reflections of irrational or socially unacceptable parts of himself. Part of the problem is that most of us are never taught how to think clearly about the sources of our own behavior and emotional distress.

The hard-driving, competitive, coronary-prone executive may tell himself and others that he is "burned out" on external success and financial gain as goals in living, that he needs to learn to relax and tune in to some very different values. He believes, he says, that money and success are far less important values than relaxation, being with people, and cultivating an inner life. The trouble is that, like all of us, he is capable of believing two (or more) incompatible things at the same time. He may also believe that not reaching his earlier high goals of money and success will leave him feeling empty, insecure, and inferior, and cause him to be esteemed much less by the important people in his life. When he tries to relax, he begins to feel vaguely threatened. A half-conscious image of himself as "on the sidelines of life" troubles and goads him. He fights the tension and worry by telling himself that he knows he is doing the right thing by cutting back on work and spending more time with his children, and that he should not worry about the consequences. The battle of reason and emotion is under way. The only certain outcome is that he will lose the war.

Many times, however, stress is not so much a product of inner conflict as of sheer, grinding frustration. Partly because we lack a useful psychological perspective on stress and human behavior, sincere attempts to more effectively manage stress in daily living are painfully unsuccessful. We live in a complex age with very little in the way of instinct or tradition to guide us. A middle-class young person growing up in the present day learns a host of intellectual and practical skills that make it possible for him or her to survive and function reasonably effectively at school, at work, and in the marketplace. But no one systematically teaches her or him absolutely essential skills in living that are needed for thinking constructively about and coping with the wide variety of stressful situations that abound in contemporary life. All of us who survive and retain a measure of sanity in the present day have learned important things about coping with stress.

The trouble is that in order to survive each of us has to reinvent the wheel. We learn a few things about coping with tension on our own, usually under conditions unfavorable for learning. We lack a common set of terms to describe our efforts at coping, and we lack the opportunity to share and refine our understandings and skills.

The first purpose of this book is to provide the reader with a useful perspective on stress and behavior. Our overstressed condition is not a senseless or chaotic one. There are reasons why we find ourselves, why we over and over again put ourselves, in this predicament. We can make psychological sense out of our fruitless worry, our anxious and hostile feelings, our excessively driven and competitive behavior, and our wheel-spinning attempts to cope with these painful effects of stress. Recent developments in clinical and social psychology have made a good beginning toward producing an understanding of the nature of stress and our attempts to cope with it. We shall endeavor to convey this understanding to you in a clear and useful fashion.

The second major purpose of this book is—in every way possible through the medium of the printed page—to help you cope more effectively with stress. The authors are clinical psychologists who have come in recent years to see a large part of their practice of psychotherapy as a rather straightforward educational enterprise. Much of psychotherapy, when it is effective, consists of providing clear and useful information concerning common problems in living, and teaching skills in coping with those problems. Much of this information, and specific, detailed descriptions of many of the strategies and tactics of coping with problems in living, can be presented in writing. Our clinical experience with such excellent self-help books as *A New Guide to Rational Living* by Albert Ellis and Robert Harper has convinced us that a curious reader, willing to experiment with new ideas and approaches, can benefit greatly from descriptions of coping techniques. We are all far more alike than we are different. Many of the problems and challenges we face are similar, as they result from our common human condition.

Our program for reducing stress involves the teaching and learning of skills in relaxation, skills in self-assertion, skills in improving interpersonal relationships, skills in rational problem solving, skills in increasing spontaneity and enjoyment, and skills in accurately assessing one's effectiveness in all these areas of functioning.

We label these skills those of stress management. We call our program Stress Management Training. We use the term *management* because it implies both thought and action. For in order to cope effectively with stress, we must learn not only to become aware of and alter some of our basic assumptions, but also to be ready to experiment with new behavior as well.

Before we begin our campaign against stress we will seek to know our opponent well. We will begin by examining, in the next chapter, the physical consequences of living with too much stress.

stress and physical disorders

The relationship between mind and body has intrigued and perplexed philosophers and scientists for centuries. An entire field, psychophysiology, is devoted to studying the effects of psychological processes on the body's physiological systems. A branch of medical science, psychosomatic medicine, is concerned with the many instances when psychological processes produce physical disease. In this chapter we shall discuss the nature and development of several diseases that are due in part to the debilitating effects of psychological stress.

Evidence is accumulating that stress reactions are likely to occur in certain environments. The effects of some environments in which threat is realistic and undeniable (such as a wartime city under siege) may be so overwhelming as to produce stress in virtually everyone exposed to them. Most environments, however, produce variable effects. Some people react with stress, while others seem to suffer no ill consequences. Some people are more susceptible to stress than others. Much medical research into psychosomatic disease has usually examined average disease rates associated with particular environments or personality types. We will summarize some of this research as it pertains to four vital health areas: hypertension, coronary disease, viruses and infections, and ulcers. This kind of research demonstrates only that certain factors are associated with stress, without explaining why those factors should produce stress in the first place. Stress reactions, as we pointed out in the previous chapter, result from an interaction between the environment and a person's appraisal of it. If the environment is seen as threatening, an individual is likely to respond with either fear or anger and the accompanying physiological arousal. Specifically, in terms of our model, we would expect that environments to which individuals are likely to react with either hostility or anxiety would be those associated with high rates of stress-produced diseases.

Stress and High Blood Pressure

Hypertension, or high blood pressure, is a silent but deadly disease that afflicts approximately one out of every five American adults. Hypertension develops slowly over the years and often produces no noticeable symptoms until it is in advanced stages. This condition of increased fluid pressure within the coronary arteries can damage the heart and kidneys, is a direct cause of strokes, and is a prime contributor to hardening of the arteries. This serious health problem has as one of its major causes psychological stress.

You probably recall that one of the accompaniments of the fight-or-flight response is an elevation of blood pressure. There is much evidence that individuals experiencing the kinds of stress that produce this arousal reaction show temporary increases in blood pressure. If the stress is intense and prolonged, the temporary elevation of blood pressure may be maintained after the stress is over, becoming a permanent increase.

The research literature abounds with examples of the ability of psychological stress to produce a hypertensive pattern. Ten years ago a Swedish research team working with rats implanted electrodes in the hypothalamus region of the brain, which controls the fight-or-flight response. In this fashion the arousal response could be turned on artifically by passing an electric current through the rats' brains. Rats whose arousal reactions were repeatedly elicited in this fashion developed and maintained elevated blood pressure. Rats not subjected to the electrical stimulation did not develop hypertension.

During the siege of Stalingrad during the Second World War, the citizens of that city were subjected to three years of bloodshed and brutality. While the fate of the city and its inhabitants hung in the balance those many months, the proportion of individuals with high blood pressure rose from about 4 percent to 64 percent. For the most part, the affected individuals continued to manifest a hypertensive pattern after the Nazi defeat. Followup studies have shown that they, as a group, did not reach their normal life expectancies.

For some years hypertension has been a major health problem of black Americans. Recent studies have indicated that high blood pressure among blacks is most probably a direct result of the stressful and demoralizing conditions of life in the ghetto. A study of black residents of middle-class neighborhoods revealed a hypertension rate one-half that of their ghetto counterparts. Black women in rural Mississippi are no more susceptible to hypertension than white women of the same socioeconomic status. Hypertension among blacks in unurbanized parts of Africa is unheard of. The implication is clear: Stressful living conditions can cause hypertension. What environment is more likely to create perpetual anger, frustration, and fear than the ghetto, with its violence, overcrowding, lack of family and economic stability, and hopelessness?

One of the most highly stressed of all groups is air traffic controllers. This psychologically demanding work, in which a mistake can result in great loss of life, has long had a reputation for debilitating those who attempt it. Not surprisingly a study revealed that air traffic controllers have an incidence of hypertension five times greater than would be expected in a comparable group.

Stress and Coronary Disease

Coronary disease is much publicized and much feared. Despite its prominent place in the consciousness of our contemporary society, heart disease was quite uncommon in this country as late as the 1920s. Since that time, it has become so widespread that more Americans now die each year from heart attacks than from any other single cause. In the public mind heart disease is linked with hereditary predisposition, improper diet, cigarette smoking, and lack of exercise. Until recently, there was little evidence that psychological factors played an important part in the development of the disease. The results of recent research now point strongly to stress as a significant contributor to the development of heart disease.

There are several different physiological events that share the common name "heart attack," all of which appear to be caused by a disease known as arteriosclerosis. Arteriosclerosis (literally "mush in the arteries") results from the adherence of fatty substances in the blood to the walls of our arteries. These fatty deposits concentrate into globs, or plaques, and become calcified and hard. This process eventually causes the arteries to become narrower and less elastic, reducing the supply of blood to the heart. Less blood in the heart means less oxygen. An inadequate supply of oxygen to the heart for a prolonged period of time can result in a myocardial infarction—the death of heart muscle tissue. A myocardial infarction also results when the blood flow to the heart is stopped entirely. Arteriosclerosis can cause this to happen in several ways. Firstly, the fatty plaques can entirely close off a coronary artery. Secondly, blood clots that tend to form around the fatty deposits may stop up one of the coronary arteries. Thirdly, pieces of plaque and the blood clot that has formed around it may break off from the arterial wall and be pumped into a branch of the coronary artery system through which it is too big to pass. There it sticks like a plug, blocking all blood flow to a portion of the heart.

At the root of arteriosclerosis seems to be the level of fats in the blood. Two of the most important of these fatty substances are cholesterol and triglycerides. There is evidence that the level of these substances in the blood is a direct function of stress. The effect of sudden stress seems to be to raise triglyceride levels, while elevations in serum cholesterol seem to follow more prolonged stress. In a study of race car drivers, it was found that their triglyceride levels were greatly elevated immediately before and during a race. Even three hours after the race the triglycerides remained at double the normal level. Studies of tax accountants show that their levels of serum cholesterol begin to rise as the April 15 tax deadline nears and begin to fall in May and early June.

In the research on coronary disease there is much evidence to support our contention that stressful environments create their damage by too often stimulating the physiological arousal of the fight-or-flight response. Not only does arousal increase the amount of fatty substance in the blood, but it also causes other changes that can lead to arteriosclerosis. There is an increased tendency of the blood to form clots. Rapidly clotting blood is a boon to a person who has been wounded in a fight but, as we have seen, blood clots can also form within the coronary arteries. Another aspect of the fight-or-flight response is the infusion of cortisone into the bloodstream. Experiments have shown that excesses of cortisone, particularly when accompanied by nervous tension, can damage the heart muscle.

Perhaps the most promising research into the psychological causes of heart disease has been summarized by Meyer Friedman and Ray H. Rosenman. They present data that suggest that personality factors or life styles may be prime contributors to coronary disease. Their research has prompted them to suggest that there is a coronary-prone behavior pattern—one that has little to do with diet or exercise. The coronary-prone individual, Type A, tends to be driven by his ambition and a sense of urgency. He is aggressive, self-demanding, impatient, and always in a hurry. He is characterized by hostility and a tendency to feel continuous pressure to accomplish. In short, these are individuals who are under constant stress.

The Type B personality is the antithesis of Type A. The Type B individual is less competitive, less rushed, and more genuinely easygoing. He is more able to loaf, to separate work from play, and less prone to anger. Very importantly, the Type B personality is relatively free from the sense of time urgency. He does not always feel rushed and impatient.

Types A and B are different in other ways as well. Type A men are *seven* times as likely to develop coronary disease as Type B men. Type A have higher cholesterol and triglyceride levels. It takes longer for A's to eliminate from their blood cholesterol added to it by a meal. The clotting elements in the blood of Type A individuals show a greater tendency to form within the coronary arteries the deadly deposits mentioned earlier. Yet another dangerous condition associated with Type A behavior is an excess accumulation if insulin in the blood. It has long been known that any physical condition associated with the excessive level of blood insulin leads to arteriosclerosis.

While the research into the deleterious effects of Type A behavior presents a convincing case for psychological stress as an important contributor to coronary disease, there is still other evidence linking stress and coronary disease. Earlier in this chapter we saw how stress can cause hypertension. Hypertension is another of the several factors that predispose individuals to heart disease. Certain changes in life style seem to bring with them a greater incidence of heart attacks. Frequent job changes are associated with increases in coronaries. Individuals who leave rural areas to take white collar employment in a city increase their risk of heart disease several times. Similarly, the urbanization of rural areas is paralleled by a rise in the incidence of coronary disease. A prime example of this pattern is the town of Roseto, Pennsylvania. Roseto was once remarkable for its abnormally low rate of heart attacks, this despite a diet abnormally high in cholesterol. The inhabitants of the town, who had immigrated from Italy, lived much as their ancestors had for generations. Investigators attributed the good health of the town to its communal spirit and the stability of its culture. This state of affairs was not to persist, however. During the 1960s changing economic forces transformed Roseto into a modern American town. As the pace of life increased and many of the old customs and traditions began to break down, so too did the health of its people. As the town became more modern, the coronary rate rose dramatically.

Stress and Immunity to Infection

The body's immunological system is necessary for our survival. We are constantly exposed to armies of microscopic invaders, capable of causing illness and even death if allowed to enter the body unopposed. The body defends itself via two primary mechanisms—inflammation and specific immunity. When foreign microbes enter the body, the tissue around them becomes inflamed, sealing them off and preventing their spread into the bloodstream. Thus surrounded, the invading microbes often can be destroyed by white blood cells. When the foreign microbes are capable of surviving the inflammatory reaction, we must rely for defense on specific immunity. Specific immunity refers to the ability of the body to identify and destroy material foreign to it. This is achieved through a rather complicated process of molecular discrimination involving the body's supply of immunoglobulin molecules, also known as antibodies. Invading microbes eventually encounter the antibodies that have complementary shapes and electrical charges. The antibodies attach themselves to the intruders, walling them off from nutrients and starving them. The body then begins to manufacture great quantities of the needed antibodies. If the invasion is massive, it may take days or even weeks to produce enough antibodies to destroy all the intruders.

It has long been a truism that tired, overworked, run-down people are highly susceptible to infections. We understand the mechanisms that affect the immunity screen well enough to know that stress and our familiar nemesis, the fight-or-flight response, make the immunity system less effective. The fight-or-flight response, you remember, involves the activation of portions of the brain stem, which cause the pituitary gland to stimulate the adrenals to secrete glucocorticoid hormones into the blood. The person under stress whose fight-or-flight response is aroused too frequently will have an excess of these hormones in his blood much of the time. We now know that an excess of these steroids impairs the effectiveness of the immunity system. These hormones reduce the power of inflammatory response and cause the body to manufacture fewer antibodies. The impaired efficiency of these two defenses makes it not only more likely that an individual will contract a disease, but also that the illness will last longer and be more severe. Experiments have shown that viruses injected into laboratory animals become many times more lethal when cortisone is injected simultaneously.

Many of us harbor in our bodies an array of microorganisms that are exceptionally virulent. Most of the time we can host these potentially deadly microbes with immunity. What then causes us to become sick? An answer that is given increasingly is stress. A study was conducted that closely observed the blood serum of twenty-four women during a flu season. The researchers discovered that the extent of flu virus present in the women's blood had little to do with their contracting the flu. Some women showed great concentrations of flu virus in their blood without becoming ill, while those who developed symptoms were often not as heavily infected. What did seem to be important in bringing on the disease was the presence of recent and debilitating stress. The women who became ill tended to have undergone unpleasant emotional experiences just prior to the onset of their flu symptoms.

The fact that disease can be brought on by stressful life experiences was documented by Doctors Holmes and Rahe of the University of Washington Medical School. They devised an inventory of forty-three life change events that have been found to be important precursors of illness. Their Social Readjustment Scale has been found to be a remarkably effective predictor of the onset of disease and disability. Each of the events on the scale has a score which corresponds to its deleterious effect on health. To use the inventory (reprinted below), you simply indicate events which have occurred during the previous year of your life. Then add the score values for each of the applicable items to make a total score of Life Change Units. Early research indicated that a person with a score of less than 150 has a 37 percent probability of becoming ill within the subsequent two years. A score of greater than 150, but less than 300, rates a 51 percent chance of illness. A score in excess of 300 means that the chances are eight out of ten that you will develop an illness over the next twenty-four months.

Social Readjustment Rating Scale*

Rank	Life event	LCU value
1.	Death of spouse	100
2.	Divorce	73
3.	Marital separation	65

* Social Readjustment Rating Scale first published in *Journal of Psychosomatic Research*, II, 213-218, 1967. Copyright 1967, Pergamon Press, Inc.

Social Readjustment Rating Scale

(continued)

Rank	Life event	LCU value
4.	Jail term	63
5.	Death of close family member	63
6.	Personal injury or illness	53
7.	Marriage	50
8.	Fired from job	47
9.	Marital reconciliation	45
10.	Retirement	45
11.	Change in health of family member	44
12.	Pregnancy	40
13.	Sex difficulties	39
14.	Gain of new family member	39
15.	Business readjustment	39
16.	Change in financial state	38
17.	Death of close friend	37
18.	Change to different line of work	36
19.	Change in number of arguments with spouse	35
20.	Mortgage over $10,000	31
21.	Foreclosure of mortgage or loan	30
22.	Change in responsibilities at work	29
23.	Son or daughter leaving home	29
24.	Trouble with in-laws	29
25.	Outstanding personal achievement	28
26.	Wife begins or stops work	26
27.	Begin or end school	26
28.	Change in living conditions	25
29.	Revision of personal habits	24
30.	Trouble with boss	23
31.	Change in work hours or conditions	20
32.	Change in residence	20
33.	Change in schools	20
34.	Change in recreation	19

35.	Change in church activities	19
36.	Change in social activities	18
37.	Mortgage or loan less than $10,000	17
38.	Change in sleeping habits	16
39.	Change in number of family get-togethers	15
40.	Change in eating habits	15
41.	Vacation	13
42.	Christmas	12
43.	Minor violations of the law	11

Some recent research has indicated that it is not merely the amount of change *per se* that predicts illness, but also the desirability of the change. Thus change that we desire or experience as positive is not significantly related to disease and disability. Changes we do not desire, however, do accumulate to create psychological distress and physical illness.

Stress and Ulcers

In addition to causing hypertension and coronary disease, and facilitating the onset of infectious diseases, stress has been linked to many other physical disorders. Of these, none is so identified with stress in the public mind as the peptic ulcer. The stereotype of the hard-driving businessman living his high-pressure life and nursing his ulcer along the way is a part of American folklore bearing considerable resemblance to reality. For the evidence is conclusive that psychological stress can and does lead to serious disorders of the digestive system.

A peptic ulcer is created when the juices of digestion burn a hole in the lining of the stomach or duodenum. The enzymes and hydrochloric acid that aid digestion in the stomach are also secreted in times of emotionality. These substances, when present in an empty stomach for prolonged periods, being to digest the stomach lining itself. Stress leading to anger is effective in stimulating the secretion of the stomach acid that causes ulcers.

One of the most intensive and illuminating studies of the human stomach was conducted by Dr. Stewart Wolf. For years he was able to study the stomach functions of a patient who, because of an injury to his esophagus, had to be fed through a surgically created opening in his abdomen. This opening also allowed the direct observation of the patient's stomach functions. These observations showed that when the patient responded to stress with an angry emotional response, excessive amounts of acid and enzymes were secreted. Numerous other laboratory studies have shown that the amount of stomach acid increases significantly when individuals are under stress.

Stress ulcers have been observed for centuries. There are documents describing a high incidence of ulcers in Roman soldiers during especially difficult military campaigns. Since the nineteenth century, physicians have recorded acute peptic ulcers in patients who had undergone the rigors of severe burns or major surgery. German air raids on English cities brought on an increase in the incidence of ulcers.

Laboratory research has shown that the predictability of an unpleasant consequence is an important factor in determining how stressful the consequence is. In a recent experiment electrodes were attached to the tails of three rats. One rat was shocked periodically, but each of the shocks was preceded by a signal that warned of the oncoming shock. A second rat received the same shocks as the first but received no reliable indication of when the shocks would occur. The third rat was attached to the experimental apparatus in the same fashion as the other two but received neither signals nor shocks. The results of the study were clear. Although both rats that were shocked developed more serious stomach ulcers than the rat which was not shocked, the rat which was given the signal that allowed it to "predict" when the shock would occur fared much better than the rat which received unpredictable shocks.

Even if one is very conservative in evaluating the available evidence, the list of physical maladies in which stress probably plays a role is quite long. Migraine headaches, backaches, asthma, constipation, acute dermatitis, menstrual pain, colitis, diarrhea, diabetes, arthritis, and even cancer have been linked to stress. It is clear that stress is a serious problem, which we have a considerable stake in combating. But the detrimental effect of stress upon body tissue is only part of the story. As we shall see in the next chapter, our environment and the view we take of it is central to many psychological and psychiatric problems as well.

stress and anger

This was an important day for Lou. He was scheduled to present his division's quarterly report at the sales meeting and woke up determined to make the day go smoothly. But the morning had started badly. The blue suit he had planned to wear was not back from the cleaners. Lou mentioned something to his wife about "letting him down" and they exchanged angry words. At the breakfast table the children were battling over a piece of toast. Lou's blood always boiled when the kids were unruly at the table. After much shouting they were quieted. On the way to work he dropped his car off to be repaired and after waiting for twenty minutes in a line of customers, he was told that there was no record of his appointment. Extremely irritated, he convinced the reluctant service manager to accept the car for servicing. Already late for work, Lou was further delayed when he had to wait another fifteen minutes for his dealer's courtesy car. By this time Lou was fuming. His schedule for the day was to be extremely hectic. At work there were some last-minute touches to be added to the sales report. Walking in the door, he discovered the place was freezing; the office heating unit had malfunctioned. Lou slammed his fist down on the desk so hard he winced from the pain. He thought to himself, "How in the name of God am I expected to get anything done when . . ."

Most of us can identify with some part of Lou's story. Getting angry when events seem to frustrate, disappoint, or abuse us is an extremely common reaction. Feeling annoyance at ourselves or other people is a regular part of many people's lives. Some of us even place a high value on being the kind of angry and aggressive personality who will allow no one to take advantage of him. The list of media events that have glorified anger and aggressiveness is endless. In our culture males who are quick to anger often are thought of as more virile and "manly" than calmer, more reasonable individuals.

Despite our tendency to glorify anger and aggressive behavior, anger is perhaps the most destructive of all emotions. It is at the root of much interpersonal conflict and unhappiness. It precipitates fights and is central in ruining many relationships. But the disruptive effect of anger on social relationships is only part of the story. In addition to alienating other people, anger can destroy our bodies from within. The angry person often is a person in danger—in danger of debilitating illness and early death.

As in the case of the other emotions we associate with stress (fear and anxiety), anger is in many respects an obsolete emotion. We rarely need to mobilize the resources of the body to physically seize territory, battle for status, or defend against attack. In our contemporary world when we get angry we usually do one of two things: (1) suppress the feeling, thus being forced to "stew in our own juices"; or (2) lash out at others, thereby damaging our relationships. From the standpoint of reducing stress neither of these options is very desirable. What does make sense for most of us is to reduce our tendencies to become angry in the first place.

Remember that the anger and arousal precipitated by stress are always the direct result of the way we perceive the world. For us to experience anger we must first have formed an appraisal of our experience that suggests that an angry or aggressive response to the environment is called for. For example, let us say you have made arrangements to meet a friend for lunch and she does not show up. If you know your friend is not forgetful and never late, you may begin to feel concerned for her safety. While waiting for a less punctual and more absentminded friend, however, the chances are greater that you will feel irritation. The difference in emotion is solely a result of placing a different interpretation on the situation. With the punctual friend we think, "She would only be late if something unavoidable had happened to delay her." While with the other friend we may think, "She is terribly thoughtless and inconsiderate."

Let us take another example. Suppose you are a five-foot ten-inch, 170-pound male. While standing in line at a theater someone shoves you from behind and says, "Move over, you jerk, you're standing on my foot." You quickly turn around and confront a scowling five-foot three-inch, 120-pound man. The chances are that you will be quite annoyed and angry. Now imagine the same situation, except that when you whirl around to confront your antagonist, he is about six feet, six inches tall and weighs about 260 pounds. What happened to the anger? Unless you hold a black belt in karate, you will feel no anger, only fear. The differing emotional responses in these two situations are again the result of differing appraisals. In both situations your rights had been infringed upon and your territory violated. The emotional difference resulted from the fact that in the first situation your brain quickly "sized up" your antagonist as presenting little or no threat to you, while in the second situation your brain's quick appraisal would read "danger."

Emotions change as quickly as do our appraisals of a situation. Let us assume that, in the first situation, you had angrily and confidently confronted your five-foot three-inch adversary, telling him that he'd better mind his manners, or else. Suppose he quickly produced a revolver from his pocket. What happens to the anger? It is replaced by the emotion of fear which matches the appraisal of probable harm. Suppose he points the gun at your head, pulls the trigger, and splashes you in the face with a stream of water. You would then undoubtedly feel relieved, perhaps even amused. The feelings of relief follow the appraisal, "I have escaped from danger."

For the most part the emotions we experience are a direct reflection of our perception of the world at the time we experience the emotion. When we feel an emotion it is because we have formed an opinion about the world that prompts that emotion. Emotions derive from acts of understanding and acts of perception. When we experience the emotion of anger it is usually in response to one or more of the following perceptions:

1. *Infringement:* Someone or something has violated our psychological territory or detracted from our status or self-worth. Unpleasant or painful intrusions into our psychological space are especially provocative of anger. An example of a violation of psychological space would be a neighbor having a noisy party while you are trying to sleep. Our status or self-esteem is part of our psychological territory. For example, we usually become angry if we hear that someone has spread malicious gossip about us.

2. *Frustration:* When we are prevented from getting something we want or are compelled to experience something unpleasant, we often respond with anger. Interference with our activities which we view as negative commonly produces anger. This is especially true when there is some person (even ourselves) whom we construe to be the agent of our misfortune.

3. *Wrongfulness and Intentionality:* Anger regularly flows from a perception of injustice or inequity. We are more likely to be angry at someone if we see his actions as wrong and intentional. If you receive a speeding ticket when, in fact, you were exceeding the speed limit, you will likely consider the punishment justified and be angry only at yourself because you "should not" have been so careless. Actions we see as both unjustified and intentional tend to make us especially angry. Conversely, when harm comes to us we always are much more ready to forgive if we learn that the harm was accidentally caused. The distinction between murder and manslaughter (and the punishment attached to each) reflects the importance we ascribe to "bad intentions."

Because anger results from perceptions of infringement or interference, reducing the frequency and intensity of angry feelings can be accomplished when we reduce our tendency to perceive the world in these ways. There are certain styles of thinking and living that are likely to predispose us to feel infringed upon, frustrated, wronged, or threatened. During the remainder of this chapter we will discuss those ways of being-in-the-world that make us vulnerable to anger. As you read the next few pages, see to what extent your life is characterized by the following anger-producing factors:

1. *Extensive Personal Boundaries:* By this expression we mean having too much on the line in too many places. Some of us allow our egos to expand and absorb so many institutions, places, roles, and people that we become vulnerable in too many areas. When one has excessive pride in everything with which one is associated, it is likely that one's pride will be offended often. Overidentification with our work, our hobbies, and our friends causes us to take personally many events that really need not cause us to feel intense emotion. The person who is perpetually angry over the performance of his favorite pro football team is confusing his team's fortunes with his own. The person who responds with anger when someone berates a friend, may be blurring the distinction between their own reputation and that of their friend. It is one thing to prefer that our favorite teams win, or to be loyal to our friends. However, when we react with anger to events that are fundamentally inconsequential to us, we make a grave error. We physiologically arouse ourselves by responding defensively to an event that, in reality, does not threaten us. In a real sense, the more things in this world we choose to identify with, the more territory we have staked out for ourselves. If your psychological space constitutes a vast empire of people, products, organizations, favorite foods, musical tastes, and countless other things, it is very likely that invasions of your territory will be daily, or even hourly, happenings.

2. *Competitiveness:* Too much has been written about the competitive orientation of American society for that material to need repeating here. From the standpoint of mental and physical well-being, our culture is clearly

*over*competitive. We know from research that competition leads to conflicts over status, money, privileges, and power. This is true for relationships with coworkers, friends, and family. A competitive orientation is often based on the assumption that victory brings happiness and that defeat means misery. This assumption is partially true for those who have their self-esteem on the line in every life situation. But the pleasure derived from victory has been highly overrated. The satisfaction of victory is always transitory; there is inevitably another contest to be waged and possibly lost.

Winning and losing, however, are not the only two alternatives that life presents us with. We can also choose the alternative of not making our lives into a series of contests. This is not to say that one must stand on the sidelines of life to lessen one's competitiveness. It is possible for each of us to find activities, relationships, and values that are, in themselves, meaningful and fulfilling. In so doing we reduce the need for competitiveness and place both our victories and our losses in their proper perspective.

3. *Moralistic Thinking:* More times than not when we are angry it is because someone has violated some rule of conduct that we believe to be true or valid. If you learn that a friend has revealed something unfavorable about you to your boss, you may be angry over the possible impact on your career. It is likely, however, that much of your anger will be in the form of blame and moral indignation. This is because you probably believe in the rule that "Friends should not spread malicious gossip." The act is especially reprehensible and irritating because it is in violation of this rule. Thus, it is often the case that we are angry at people when they do things we believe they should not have done, or when they do not do things they should have done. To summarize, anger often comes from perceiving the violations of a moral rule.

The more your thinking is characterized by *shoulds* and *should nots* the more likely it is that events will provoke anger in you. Does this mean that we must abandon our ethical positions in order to reduce stress?

Not at all. What must be abandoned is moralizing rather than morality. Most of us have values that are very important to us, which we could not sacrifice without giving up something very important about ourselves. It is one thing to decide for ourselves what we believe to be right and wrong. It is quite another to attempt to impose those beliefs on others. It is when we attempt to legislate the conduct of others that we make ourselves most susceptible to anger. The first step in counteracting the effects of moralistic thinking is learning to accept the fact that what you believe is just that, what you believe, and is subject to some doubt and uncertainty. Unless you are in the extraordinary position of having direct revelations from a divine source, there is ample reason to proceed with caution when attempting to decide for others what they should or should not do. Tolerance is one of the most effective antidotes to hostility.

Much of what passes for moralistic thinking is really just a series of statements describing what we feel good about or prefer. Most parents of teenage children would prefer that their children respect them as wise and experienced individuals. When they elevate this preference into a piece of morality, however, they create trouble for themselves. The great likelihood that teenagers will not see their parents in this light sets the moralizing parent up for continual frustration and feelings of moral indignation. Learning to change "You should" into "I want" is an important step, not only to lowering hostility but also toward improving interpersonal relations.

Moralizing is a roadblock to identifying with and understanding the other person's frame of reference. There is a French saying: "Whatever can be understood can be forgiven." Empathy, understanding, and forgiveness are essential qualities to cultivate if you wish to make yourself less vulnerable to anger.

4. *Attributional Thinking:* We are all engaged in an effort to make some sense out of the world around us. We continually try to understand the causes of our behavior as well as the behavior of others. Research has demonstrated that our way of explaining the actions of others is often very different from the way we explain our own

behavior. We think of our own behavior as being caused by our immediate circumstances, while we see the behavior of others as resulting from their enduring intentions and dispositions. Suppose your spouse says angry words to you and you reply in kind. When asked for your analysis of the situation you would probably say that he attacked you and intended to hurt your feelings, whereas you were only responding in kind to his initial provocation. His view of the interchange also would probably describe his harsh words as caused by something you had done to him, and your words as stemming from your intention to hurt.

When we see the other person's negative behavior to be a consequence of his or her intentions or intrinsic qualities, we are much more likely to respond with anger. You will recall that negative behavior that is seen as accidental is less likely to lead to anger. We are never angrier than when we believe another's behavior to be based soley on malicious intent. Of course, this is almost never the case. Any behavior is always caused by a complex set of circumstances. Even in the rare instances when true, premeditated, malicious intent is present, our anger is softened by understanding, from the other's point of view, how those malicious feelings developed. Thus, focusing on the intentions or personality traits we believe to have been responsible for the behavior we dislike makes us more prone to anger. It also makes us more likely to judge and be angry at the whole person rather than the specific behavior. Learning to take the other person's perspective, to put yourself in the other person's shoes, is a great help in realizing that the behavior of others usually seems as justified to them as your behavior does to you. Focusing on the big picture, the varied multitude of personal, social, intentional, unintentional, lasting, circumstantial, psychological, and physical factors that go into producing any piece of behavior, can make us more understanding, tolerant, and forgiving people.

5. *Low Tolerance for Frustration and Discomfort:* Hostile people are often those who in some real sense have not achieved psychological maturity. They react to the

normal, inescapable discomforts of life with outrage and indignation. Many people react as though they believe that they deserve to get what they want and have the right to be free from discomfort. Many of us (at least to some degree) think we are entitled to get what we want every time we want it. This belief is extraordinarily perfectionistic and unrealistic in addition to being self-defeating. But many people hold this kind of belief without even knowing it.

A patient of ours used to see red every time he was held up in a traffic jam entering the Holland Tunnel. One day I asked him if he expected to drive his whole life without being stalled by congested traffic. He answered, "Of course not."

"But each time you're stuck in traffic you react as though you've been ripped off, undeservedly thwarted by fate. Instead of saying to yourself, 'Oh yes, this is one of the times I don't get through the tunnel without a long wait,' you say, 'This shouldn't be happening to me.' "

"Right. So what?"

"If you think 'This shouldn't happen' each time it happens, then it means you believe it should never happen."

"I never really thought about it that way."

The patient's unarticulated belief, "I should never have to wait," made his hostility inevitable.

In both the case of our patient and in your case, the beliefs that lead to stress can be changed. In Part 2 of this book we will present methods that will enable you to reorient your thinking so as to reduce the stress in your life.

In this chapter we have covered the "fight" part of the fight-or-flight response that is aroused by stress. Before we move on to a discussion of the "flight" or anxiety reaction, we shall take this opportunity to emphasize once again certain features of the relationships among stress, arousal, anger, and anxiety. Stress is an expectation of future harm or discomfort. Arousal is the physical and emotional activation that accompanies the belief that something bad is about to happen to us. We are aroused both when we are angry and when we are anxious. Anger results from feeling infringed upon or frustrated, especially by a wrongful action. Anger is an emotion felt when we are removed by distance or time from the possibility of real harm. It is an emotion associated with dominance, power, and confidence. Anxiety, on the other hand, is the emotion of danger. We feel anxiety when we believe harm is about to befall us, when we feel unable to protect ourselves. The more immediate and serious the danger, the greater is the anxiety felt. In the next two chapters we will turn to a discussion of this emotion, which has been said to characterize the modern age.

4

stress and
anxiety

What Is Anxiety?

The best place to start looking for an answer to this question is with the everyday observation that different persons will react in enormously different ways to virtually the same stressful situation. A situation like being host at a social gathering will elicit calm, outgoing, task-oriented behavior in one person, painful anxiety, tension, and worry in someone else, and cause a third person to develop such severe stomach cramps that the party has to be cancelled. What we have here is not so much one calm and two anxious individuals as three persons who are equally exercising their native human capability to decide for themselves what is really happening in this situation and how they wish to feel about it.

In such a situation the anxious person selectively notices only periods of awkward silence in conversation as the evening begins, while the calm individual notices quiet, relaxed looks of interest and anticipation. The anxious person judges that his activities as host are somehow responsible for a particular guest's sullen, unpleasant mood and behavior, and further believes that this unpleasantness reflects negatively on his basic worth or attractiveness as a human being. The unanxious host wonders what the sullen guest's problem is, is friendly but does not try extra hard to entertain him, and reflects that if there is any stuff to him at all he will probably call the next day with an apology and explanation for his behavior.

The calm individual may end the party with feelings of increased confidence and pleasure in himself and the situation, while the anxious one ends up feeling inferior, personally devastated, and helplessly victimized by a stressful situation and anxious feelings. Both of them, however, exerted enormous and far-reaching influence on their own feelings, mood, and behavior. They may not know for sure how they did it, or how (if desired) to change what they did to produce different feelings and results. But both actively created their own pain or pleasure, their own anxious or calm feelings.

The emotional state of anxiety is a composite of feeling and physiology. On the subjective side, anxiety is a unique kind of feeling state that is qualitatively different from other emotional states such as grief, anger, or sorrow. It is characterized by varying amounts of feelings of apprehension, dread, terror, or nervousness. On the more objective or behavioral side it is marked by heightened autonomic nervous system activity and such symptoms as heart palpitation, sweating, disturbances in breathing, and the tensing of muscles.

Feelings of anxiety and physical symptoms like muscle tension and heart palpitation are an important part of the experience of anxiety. But they are on the surface or periphery of that experience. Behind these health-disrupting symptoms of anxiety is usually found a very personal kind of worried, fearful thinking. It may take the form of feverish or panicky worry about some imminent personal disaster. Or it may be painful rumination about social or work performances that do not meet up to one's own or others' standards. Or perhaps it is somber, tense plotting and replotting of ways to surmount obstacles to goals one feels one must not fail to reach. At the core of anxiety, though, is worry. By and large anxiety is worry—worry about social and financial disasters, worry about loss of self-esteem, worry about failing to reach one's goals, worry about emotional and material security in an uncertain world. Worry, especially chronic or repetitious worry, produces fearful moods, physical tension, and all the other symptoms of anxiety.

Once we understand that worry or anxious thinking lies at the core of anxiety, however, we can begin to grasp the amazing extent to which we actively self-create the stress that comes to plague us. The fact that we actively create our most important feelings and experiences gives not only hope for change, but the actual opportunity, leverage, and tools to accomplish change. The same faculties of reasoning, judgment, and imagination that lead us to regard many fairly innocuous events as serious threats or personal catastrophes can be used to reevaluate and redirect our thinking and behavior.

This certainly does not mean that a person can exert instant mind or thought control and thereby change feelings or eliminate anxiety at will. Learning how to manage thoughts and alter your environment to minimize stress may involve changing long-standing patterns of thinking and coping that will take some time and a lot of effort. Meaningful, self-directed change, however, is possible.

Dimensions of Anxious Thinking

In this section we will describe some of the processes associated with anxious thinking. We will illustrate these processes with examples from the experiences of men and women in a common contemporary stress situation, namely the stress of taking examinations.

There are several reasons for selecting test taking to illustrate worry in action. First, it is a situation with which many of us can identify. Secondly, the nature and treatment of test anxiety has been a much researched subject by psychologists in recent years; through studying it we have learned quite a bit about reactions to stress. Finally, test anxiety is in many ways a metaphor for contemporary life. We seem to face innumerable academic and social "tests" as we move through life. Many of them are potentially stressful in the sense that they appear dangerous or threatening to us. They seem dangerous because "failing" them may interfere with reaching important goals. Or they seem threatening because performing poorly tends to lower our sense of self-worth.

We can learn a great deal about the concrete reality of

stress and anxiety by putting test anxiety under the microscope. Test anxiety is usually measured by administering a questionnaire to individuals that asks them to report the degree to which they experience various signs or effects of anxiety in test-taking situations. They are asked if, in testing situations, they feel anxious or panicky, worry about themselves or their performance, or feel that anxiety interferes with their performance on tests. They are also asked if they experience difficulty in breathing, rapid heartbeat, heavy sweating, or physical tension during tests.

A number of interesting experiments have shown that students who get high scores on such a questionnaire (and therefore are highly test-anxious) do much more poorly than students with low test-anxiety scores on certain learning exercises (like first memorizing and then recalling a list of words). However, the highly test-anxious individuals do more poorly only when they are given achievement-oriented instructions before the learning task. That is, anxiety interferes with performance only when students are instructed to do as well as they can and told that the learning task is an important one that relates to intelligence or academic achievement. When the task is presented in a low-pressure manner, as merely an exercise, the highly test-anxious students do as well or better than their low anxiety counterparts. In other words, test anxiety emerges only when people believe they have something important at stake. Highly test-anxious students generally receive lower grades and drop out of college more frequently than do less anxious students of equivalent intellectual ability.

We will indicate the main dimensions of test anxiety in some detail because we believe they are present in ineffective coping with stress in many areas of living. Specifically, for our purposes, we would like to identify four main dimensions of anxious functioning that are present in most human reactions to stress. All four can be found in test anxiety, and they are:

1. *Self-Talk.* This refers to how you actively think about, interpret, and talk to yourself about stressful situations in living.
2. *Direction of Attention.* Is attention focused on your-

self and your worries, or can you lose yourself in relaxed, task-oriented attention to problems that arise?

3. *Response to Bodily Signs of Tension.* Do you respond to tension with increased worry and tension-producing effort, or can you use tension as a signal to do things that eliminate anxiety?

4. *Basic Beliefs and Assumptions.* Crucial basic beliefs may reflect either conflicted, overevaluative thinking or calm, rational thinking about potentially stressful events.

These four features of the ongoing stream of behavior are closely interconnected. For example, one's self-talk reflects basic beliefs, is important in directing attention productively, and strongly influences the nature of one's responses to bodily signs of tension.

Self-Talk

Everyone, in a very literal sense, talks to himself. What we do, and how well we do it, depends to a great extent upon what we say to ourselves.

This is most evident with children. You might patiently teach a little boy how to make something with blocks by saying to him several times, "Now you put the red block on top of the blue block, just like this, see?" If you should observe him later doing it by himself, you might well hear him say to himself out loud, "Now I put the red one on top of the blue one, see? Good boy." The instructions and praise you used with him, he now uses to talk to himself and guide his behavior. If he knocks the blocks over, you may say to him, "Oh, what the hell, you'll never get it." Later you might observe him trying it once, failing, and then angrily pushing the blocks away saying, "I'll never get it!" Already he has learned how to create negative emotions. When this child grows up and encounters frustration, he may say to himself silently, "I'll never get it . . . I knew it . . . I'm a crummy person."

Adults talk to themselves and instruct themselves, albeit silently most of the time. They carry on a rich inner dialogue of words and pictures that determines much of what they feel and do. By far, most of our experience is not direct experience of events and situations, but experience of the things we tell ourselves or imagine about these events. This inner dialogue, these self-created images of what is or might be, also determines our response to potentially stressful situations. It is never events themselves, but what we tell ourselves or imagine about them that creates fear and anxiety.

Following are some examples of anxiety-producing self-talk written down by university students immediately after taking a midterm exam. They may help to convey some of the reality and flavor of the panicky, distracting inner dialogue that lies at the core of anxiety.

I'm on a scholarship that takes a 3.0 to keep it. I hope I studied well enough not to mess that up. Oh, God, if anything happened to that, then what would I do. I'd have to pay tuition . . . I can't afford that . . . then what, then what?

Oh, my God, I don't know any of this and I studied for so long. I must be so *stupid*. I'm going to blow my whole grade on this one test. I want to drop this course. What am I going to do . . . What am I going to do? I am *really* scared.

Wow, this really looks hard! I studied that . . . why can't I remember it? I should have studied harder. How can I get that, it looks too hard! Now what? I should have studied harder!

Oh, no, multiple choice. Every time I have trouble with multiple choice tests I get sick. The last time it ruined the whole day. I'll be just sick if I have to go through that again! Why couldn't it have been some different kind of test?

I know the general idea but I'm afraid I can't get it down in concise words . . . I wonder what he wants . . . I don't know exactly what he wants. How would he grade that, there's no way to tell. Should I add something? Who knows? I wish it had been multiple choice.

Jesus, that's two questions in a row I didn't know. I feel so tight. What if I can't get the next one! Then what!

I can just see myself now, man—working in a coffee shop instead of teaching! I hope nobody gets them all right and screws up the curve!

There probably won't be enough time, there never is, damn it. My hands are so sweaty I can't hold this pen. Rush, I've got to rush . . . I just hope somebody up there's with me.

Anxious self-talk during studying or tests almost always seems to fall into one of the following five categories.

1. *Worrying about one's performance,* as compared with personal standards or how well others are doing.
2. *Ruminating over alternatives* too long and fruitlessly.
3. *Being preoccupied with bodily reactions* associated with anxiety, leading to intensified anxiety symptoms.
4. *Ruminating about imagined consequences* of doing poorly on the text—disapproval, punishment, loss of status or self-esteem, damage to academic record or job chances, etc.
5. *Thoughts and feelings of inadequacy,* including self-criticism or self-condemnation, such as calling oneself names like "stupid," etc.

These themes of worrying give us clues concerning the basic structure of anxious thinking. We will be dealing with them, at least implicitly, throughout the book. However, there are several subtle and quite devastating aspects of the process of anxious thinking we have yet to describe that show up vividly in the stressful testing situation.

Worry Is Self-Escalating. Worry is addictive. It is extremely difficult to give up, and its grip on one's thinking tends to intensify.

The self-escalating character of anxious thinking and self-talk is well illustrated by the old horse trainer's explanation of the skittishness and tendency to panic and run away exhibited by many horses. It appears that the horse just happens to be running, notices that it is running, infers that it must be running from something dangerous, starts to run faster, notices that it is running faster, infers that the danger is getting closer, begins to run faster still, and so forth.

The chain of self-escalating illogic seems to go something like this. Because one is concerned about a problem, there may be something to worry about. Because one is starting to worry, it is possible there is a serious threat at hand. Because that possibility is indeed a very serious one, more worry seems justified. And so on.

Consider a test-anxious student. She starts out with simple concern. Something might go wrong on the test. She fantasizes possible disturbing sequences of flunking the test and tells herself that they just may come to pass. Now she begins to worry about whether or not she will do well on the test and what will happen if she does not. She imagines not knowing answers, failing the exam, feeling humiliated, and doing poorly on future tests. Her imagination runs away with itself before anything bad has happened. After worrying for a bit she may tell herself that if she fights hard and is very careful she may avoid possible disasters. But by this time she has generated additional tension and concern that only seem to be more evidence for the thesis that harm is possible. There must be some danger there somewhere. Thus anxiety escalates.

The student, of course, loses sight of a very simple fact, namely, that flunking a test is virtually never harmful to a student, now or in the future. It is very rarely more than an annoyance, a small problem to be dealt with in some appropriate manner. A bad grade is a sign that there is a problem that may require attention. It tells the recipient that he or she had better stop, look, and figure out what went wrong. It is almost always possible to get accurate information concerning the answers. One test rarely ruins a single course grade, let alone a career. One may need to study more or differently, adopt a different test-taking strategy, or acquire some additional intellectual skills. If this cannot be accomplished within a reasonable period of time with an acceptable amount of hard work, then it is time to change courses, academic majors, or career directions—the sooner the better! Such a change is no more a cause for worry than a bad grade on a test. It simply calls for calm problem solving and action in a different direction, with every reason to expect a satisfactory outcome. Of course, anyone might get upset over a bad grade on a test, temporarily. But chronic, ongoing anxiety that may seriously undermine both happiness and academic performance—which is what we usually mean by stress—calls for a radical solution that gets at the root of anxious thinking.

Self-escalating worry lies at the source of our experience of anxiety and panic. However, it is important to realize that anxious thinking is not necessarily explicit or conscious. If it were, there would probably be much less of it! Psychotherapy for anxiety problems often involves helping a person become lucidly aware of how he or she is talking to him- or herself and thinking irrationally about disturbing events. Anxious thinking usually goes on under a blanket of panicky or depressed feelings that mask it and hide it from view.

The fact that we are often unaware of worried thinking plays an important role in getting anxiety started. Later on, in the teeth of intense anxiety, an individual may suddenly become aware that he or she is thinking and reacting in a very irrational manner. By then, however, it is usually too late to interrupt or get control of the process. One of the main benefits to be derived from the relaxation, meditation, and cognitive change methods described later in this book is that they can help one become aware of physical tension or worried thinking early, when it is still possible to take effective measures to counteract them.

Worry Is Self-Perpetuating. Anxious thinking is self-perpetuating. It tends to become insulated against effective reconsideration by the anxious person. What seems to happen is this. I am afraid, let us say, of being rejected by another person, or not achieving success in some endeavor, or flunking a test. The thought may occur to me that perhaps one of these things is not such a catastrophe as I seem to believe. I may even honestly wonder if it matters at all! But immediately I pull back from that thought, and do not pursue it. It seems very dangerous, like a rock near an old campfire that probably is not too hot to touch, but I am not about to find out. If I reevaluate how dangerous the situation is, I might let down my guard for even a moment. What if I decide I have nothing to worry about when there is a real chance something bad could happen to me? I might not do what I must to protect myself. Usually anxious people would rather be safe than sorry.

This kind of logic is seductive, but it is incorrect on all counts. It simply is not true that by a reconsideration of perceived threats we run any greater risk of error than in not reevaluating them. When anxious, we are not really any safer or more careful than when we are relaxed. In fact, by obsessing over immediate dangers, we very well may fail to give needed attention to important long-term consequences and thus place ourselves in real jeopardy.

Direction of Attention

All of us exert an enormous influence upon our own welfare by how we direct attention to different parts of our experience. To a great extent human freedom has to do with how and to what we direct our attention as we encounter potentially stressful events. The dynamics of attention are absolutely critical to test anxiety and to coping with stress in general.

So far as the direction of attention is concerned, the heart of the matter is a distinction between self-oriented and task-oriented thinking. *Self*-oriented thinking is self-evaluative. It is preoccupied with the self and its worries. It leads to escalating worry, anxiety, and impaired or unsatisfying performance. *Task*-oriented thinking is directed outward toward others and the world. It leads to relaxed involvement in the task, self-forgetfulness, minimal worry, and good chances for a successful and pleasant outcome. Self-oriented or self-preoccupied thinking is worried, threatened thinking. It is ruminating about feared consequences, how one compares with some standard of performance, how well one is doing compared with other people, and so forth. Task-oriented thinking is not worrying about any of these things but is instead losing oneself in the task or activity or pleasure at hand.

The highly test-anxious student directs his attention to himself and to worries about the self—how well am I doing, what will happen to me if I fail, etc. What often happens is that when a student comes to a question he cannot immediately answer, he feels that he can't remember and then begins to panic. Just at that point he focuses attention on himself. He starts thinking, "Oh, God, I don't know the answer." As

45

his anxiety grows he thinks, "I'm going to louse up this test. I may fail it. I just can't do it. I'm stupid." Such worried self-talk may become a self-fulfilling prophecy.

The unanxious student responds to the challenge of not knowing the answer to a particular question with task-oriented thinking. He does not immediately lapse into evaluating how well he is doing or is likely to do on the test, but rather focuses on the problem at hand. The problem at hand is how to make the best use of the time available to make the best grade possible on this test. Most likely he will weigh the alternatives of spending some time trying to come up with some free associations that will lead to a correct answer, or of deciding to move on to another question and return to the more difficult item when he has finished the questions that he can answer immediately. He will choose between these alternatives and probably do well no matter what he chooses. The point is that he is focused on the task. His attention is directed toward his problem, not toward himself.

Contrast our effective student with the individual who is making himself more anxious by focusing on questions such as "Am I good enough?" or "Will I be able to get into medical school?" Self-oriented thinking can also take the form of self-criticism, focusing on how anxious you are, or directing attention to the bodily signs of anxiety. Directing attention to any of these areas not only serves to increase anxiety but also keeps your attention away from where it needs to be—on how to deal effectively with whatever situation is presenting a challenge. In the case of test anxiety, students who are thinking about themselves are not able to devote full attention to the test. Consequently they do not perform up to their abilities.

To many people the term *task-oriented* may suggest a relatively impersonal stance toward persons and things. Nothing could be further from the truth. It is the self-absorbed people of this world, the people who are preoccupied with their own anxieties, who are most likely to be insensitive to the needs of others. People who are effective in their relationships with others are usually those who can pay enough attention to the other person to really have some sense of who that other person is and what he expects out of the relationship. If you are focused on your anxiety, fill your head with questions of how well you measure up, or in any way stand back from your behavior and evaluate it, you will miss much of what the other person communicates. This will tend to make you feel a little out of touch and even more unsure of yourself. All of which will make it difficult for you to act relaxed and natural. You will become even more anxious when you see yourself behave tensely and witness the fact that people are probably less responsive to you when you are uptight. The cycle is vicious and self-perpetuating. It is easier to prevent than to interrupt. Learning to direct attention toward the outside world and away from self-evaluation is an extremely important step in lowering anxiety.

Response to Bodily Tension

There are wide individual differences among people in the experience of physical and emotional tension. Some common symptoms are muscular tension (especially in the stomach and neck), headaches, nausea, rapid heartbeat or breathing, heavy sweating, and general feelings of anxiety and tension. One of the most important factors in coping with stress is how one interprets and responds to the initial signs of physical tension. Is tension interpreted as a sign that you truly must be in a threatening situation, leading to increased worry and tension? Or is it viewed as a cue or signal that you are unnecessarily allowing yourself to become overwrought, leading to the initiation of effective coping strategies to counteract stress?

If they are not coped with effectively, physical and emotional tensions tend to accelerate. The key to coping with them successfully is to become aware of bodily tension early in the process and take effective measures to deal with it at that point. Ineffective coping with physical tension usually takes one of two forms. Either we suppress our awareness of physical tension, or we try to fight it with effortful responses that only increase tension rather than reduce it.

We often feel that minor indications of bodily tension are not worth our concern. To interrupt our activities to examine the pressures we are under seems a waste of time or perhaps self-indulgent. The problem is, of course, that anxious feelings and physical tension, like anxious thinking, tend to escalate. They are a signal that unless there is some basic shift in coping strategy, tension will almost certainly increase. Physical and emotional tensions tend to become habitual reactions to stress. Their effects may be cumulative. And they may become a serious threat to health.

Tension may build to the point where it cannot be ignored any longer and some response must be made to it. What often happens then is that we make an effortful response that only increases tension rather than reduces it. The text-anxious student at this point will often try tensely to fight through the tension and anxiety, trying hard to concentrate and function in spite of them. Often people will actually tense muscles as part of their effort to try to relax. Bodily signs of tension may be interpreted as a sign that one is somehow inferior or lacks the skills to successfully meet demands. This leads to self-criticism that only makes matters worse.

Bodily signs of anxiety and tension may cause us to further tense up. But they may be viewed as cues to relax and to take a more relaxed approach to coping with stressful situations. This may involve shifting to another coping strategy that we either possess or can develop in a reasonable period of time. Making such a shift and getting involved in task-oriented thinking can quickly reduce tension. It is also useful to have in your repertoire specific tactics for coping with stress, techniques that allow you to quickly and efficiently produce mental calm and physical relaxation. The meditation, relaxation, and self-hypnosis techniques described in the second part of this book are examples of such tactics.

Basic Beliefs and Assumptions

Our model of stress has emphasized perceptions of threat rather than external events or environmental demands. It is becuase of perceptions of threat that we think anxiously and in a self-oriented manner. Ultimately our perceptions of threat are anchored in maladaptive beliefs about ourselves and the world.

What we wish to emphasize most strongly is that this kind of belief, leading to perceptions of threat, is what causes unpleasant emotional arousal. Many test-anxious persons, if you asked them what they really believed about the testing situation, would say they believe that the test is probably a fair one, that they have the ability to pass it, and that there is no

48

good reason why they should be anxious. But, they would add, feelings of tension and anxiety, sometimes gradually, sometimes suddenly, sweep over them on tests, cloud their more rational view of the situation, and disrupt their performance. They are puzzled about where these feelings come from, and frustrated because their attempts to counteract them do not seem to work. Their feelings of anxiety come in large part from a set of irrational beliefs that are incompatible with their more rational views of the test-taking situation. Such beliefs are that intense worry will improve their performance or help them avoid mistakes, that the situation is fraught with danger, that failure on the test would be an irreparable personal catastrophe and so forth. These beliefs guarantee a sense of threat, worry, and considerable emotional arousal.

Sometimes our beliefs about stressful events are simply mistaken or incorrect. More often, as in the example just given, there is conflict among beliefs or belief systems. Where such a conflict exists we are characteristically much more aware of the beliefs on one side of the conflict. Usually these beliefs are more socially acceptable for us to hold than their opposite numbers on the other side of the conflict. As we suggested in an earlier chapter, these conflicts are often viewed as a conflict between reason and emotion, and are enshrined as such in many psychological theories. In fact, this view is incorrect, and quite disastrous for the practical business of coping with stress. The conflict is between belief and belief, between value and value, with different emotions associated with each side of the conflict.

Two major problems arise when one thinks about coping with stress in terms of a conflict between reason and emotion. The first and most obvious is that we then become relatively helpless victims of invading emotional forces that arise mysteriously and uncontrollably from the unconscious or the gut. It is not clear to us where these troublesome emotions really come from, or what to do about them.

The second problem with viewing the struggle as a conflict between reason and emotion is that by thinking in terms of a conflict between reason and emotion we disown responsibility for our mistaken beliefs and their consequences. We identify reason as the "real me" that lies at the center of the self. We locate reason right in the center of the knowing, choosing, believing "I." We picture emotion as something that arises in more peripheral regions of the self. It seems less central to the "real me" than thoughts and wishes that we can often control or alter at will. But the distressing emotions associated with mistaken or contradictory beliefs are just as central or "real me" as the reason with which they supposedly conflict. To split off emotion from reason and to locate emotion in a peripheral region of the self is to put them beyond the reach of reevaluation and change.

In the next chapter we will take a detailed look at the kinds of beliefs that lead to stress and anxiety. Just as we did with anger, we will show how certain beliefs spawn certain emotions. Examining the basic assumptions that underlie anxiety will move us closer to the kinds of understanding needed to conquer stress.

5

the anatomy
of anxiety

In this chapter we will describe four kinds of anxiety-producing beliefs and try to illustrate how they are involved in everyday experiences of stress and anxiety. Mistaken beliefs that produce anxiety actually structure the world of our experience. Once we look out on the world through the lens of mistaken beliefs, events are distorted and anxiety is inevitable. To stretch the point a little, one might even say that anxiety is reasonable—when one views the world in such a distorted way. Examples of mistaken beliefs are: "I'm nobody if people don't respect me," "If I lost my girlfriend I would have nothing to live for," "To survive in the social jungle requires constant attention to people's actions and motives toward me," "I simply must be the best in my line of work, that's what it's all about," "Most people mean well, but we're forced to compete pretty viciously with each other in a dog-eat-dog world," "The worst thing that could happen to me would be to be really alone," "You can't trust people unless you have something they want," "It's best not to extend yourself unless you are fairly sure you won't get hurt," "I'm just

51

not as forceful or charming as most people and must try to make up for that by working harder."

There are a few common themes running through anxiety-producing beliefs that permit them to be grouped into a small number of very general categories. Once articulated, these themes seem to touch upon some of the deepest perennial struggles of human beings. They seem to clarify some of the issues we are fundamentally up against in matters of stress and anxiety. In this chapter we will discuss four general categories of beliefs that lie at the root of most anxiety.

The Efficacy of Worry

The first category of beliefs is made up of mistaken assumptions about thinking itself. We call these superstitious beliefs about the efficacy of worry. Many people—everyone who worries a lot—believe that active worry is an essential ingredient in their daily coping activities, one they could not eliminate without courting disaster.

Human beings have the distinctive ability to anticipate the future and allow it to mold their present behavior. We can invent the idea of something never seen before (the electric light, democracy, a spaceship), and then create it. We may be partly creatures of habit. But we are even more creatures of rational intelligence who can make plans for the future and begin to realize them in the present.

One of the most remarkable features of our rational intelligence is our ability to deal with the unfamiliar and the uncertain. How effectively we solve the problems posed for us by unfamiliar situations and unexpected events determines much of our success in realizing plans for the future. How effectively we deal with uncertainty as we try to achieve our goals for the future also determines much of our emotional welfare. The key to emotional well-being lies in how we think about unfamiliar and uncertain (i.e., potentially stressful) events.

But it is essential to draw a sharp distinction between worry or worried thinking on the one hand, and planning for the future or rational problem solving on the other. To use the terms of an earlier chapter, effective planning and problem solving involve task-oriented thinking that is not impaired by self-oriented worry about oneself and the outcomes of one's behavior. There is a qualitative difference between worry and even the most intense and serious task-oriented thinking. The remainder of this section will clarify the distinction between problem solving and worry.

When persons who worry a great deal begin to look at their own thinking patterns they usually discover many statements they make to themselves daily that express and reinforce their superstitious beliefs about worry's effectiveness. They discover that they regularly attribute successful coping with daily stresses to the presence of worry. They really believe that only because they worried about alternatives, checked things out over and over again, and nurtured the whole process along with more worry were they successful in accomplishing something positive or avoiding failure. On the other hand, when things work out badly, they often decide that this happened because they did not worry enough!

People who are anxious much of the time or in many situations are often profoundly attached to the belief that worrying keeps them alert to possible danger, or protects them from committing various moral, social, or practical errors. It is often difficult for them to seriously question their belief in the value of worrying, for fear that to stop worrying would expose them to a whole host of possible dangers. Giving up worry or a belief in its effectiveness seems like dropping one's shield in battle. Perhaps the battle has ended, but there seems to be no way to know this for certain without risking exposure to danger.

Many of us worry to a lesser degree than the chronically anxious person, and only under certain circumstances. For example, we may believe that worried preparation for a party, speech, or test is useful in avoiding social or academic disaster—or at least it may be useful, and so we had better worry. Such a belief may lead to considerable psychological tension or, paradoxically, to putting off preparation until the last moment. After all, worry makes us feel uncomfortable. Often the worried anticipation of a stressful situation, for example stage fright, is worse than the actual performance. Because anticipation and worry are so unpleasant we often delay or avoid. Worry about the things we must do demoralizes us, making it difficult to work up the motivation to get started. Much behavior that is apparently lazy or irresponsible really is based on assumptions similar to those that underlie overwork. Thus overwork and escape from work can both result from the same mistaken assumptions about the world.

Beliefs about the effectiveness of worry are superstitious in the sense that because our successes in the past have been accompanied by worry we conclude that they were caused by worry. This is no more rational than concluding that a rain dance at the beginning of the growing season causes the ensuing rains. In fact, rain dances serve constructive social and religious functions. Worry does not.

Undoing this mistaken belief about worry's effectiveness often must involve learning what specific kinds of thinking are actually helpful in dealing with stressful situations. Often we would rather not get that specific because the process disturbs some of our most ingrained habits and assumptions.

Implicit in our analysis of worrying is a very important basic principle. According to this principle there are only two kinds of problematic events or situations. There are those we can influence or control in some manner, and those we cannot influence or control. Every potentially stressful event falls into one of these two categories. One may need to divide a complex situation, like a friendship or a financial problem, into those aspects that one can change or influence and those one cannot. But once they are divided they belong wholly to one of these two mutually exclusive categories.

Consider worries about money. We can effectively control many things in the realm of personal finances. It is neither difficult nor time-consuming to keep careful track of income and expenses, assess one's needs and desires, and plan carefully and realistically for the future. Anyone can acquire these skills, and they are a superb antidote for anxiety about money. On the other hand, there are specific expenses, accidents, and shifts in the larger economic situation that no one could anticipate or control. They are unexpected, they cannot be predicted in advance, and they may create serious problems when they occur. Financial problems can be divided into two categories—those we can and those we cannot do anything about.

There are only events we can influence and events we cannot influence. Worry of any kind has absolutely no positive role to play in dealing with either type of stressful event. Worry about situations one can influence is always distracting and unproductive. It involves trying to anticipate the unpredictable, dwelling on negative outcomes that are usually highly unlikely. It involves magnifying these negative possibilities so that they become catastrophes we are helpless to prevent, instead of problems that can be solved in an efficient manner when they occur. Worry drains energy and takes attention away from things that really matter. It prevents us from enjoying life when problems are absent, and tends to prevent an objective appraisal of problems when they do arise. Worry and anxious thinking play absolutely no constructive role whatsoever in daily living.

Worry about situations that one cannot change or influence is equally unproductive. Some of these situations, like the loss of a job, a financial reversal, or the discovery that a friend or lover has negative qualities we were not aware of, may just call for simple acceptance and the shifting of attention to other matters where something positive can be accomplished. Others, like the death of someone close to us, may trigger a lengthy process of reflection about the meaning of this event that may lead to valuable philosophical deepening or growth. Such reflection may involve deep currents of feeling, from despair to elation, but normally very little anxiety is part of the process. In no case is worry or rumination fruitful.

Probably no one worries about events that they believe cannot be anticipated or controlled in any way. But we often distort our perception of uncontrollable events, resisting full acceptance of the idea that we cannot influence them. No doubt we find it difficult to acknowledge how little control we exercise over many of the things that happen to us. The more we know, the more we realize we do not really understand. The more we accomplish, the more clearly we see how it could all be quickly undone by a cruel turn of events. Notice, though, how often we worry for long periods of time about possible misfortunes, only to have our plans upset in the end by something we could never have anticipated. The worry was costly in terms of stress, and benefited us nothing.

Returning to personal finances, we often seem to believe that worrying about money accomplishes something constructive. That belief is entirely false. It is not difficult to manage money efficiently, and worry adds nothing to the process. Part of our worrying about money, no doubt, is an attempt to cope with uncertainty and protect ourselves against misfortune. But worry can provide us only with the illusion of control. In fact, unexpected problems in the realm of personal finance are just that—unexpected! It does no good at all to worry about them in advance.

Here we must make a crucial distinction between not being able to anticipate certain problems—financial or otherwise—and not being able to cope smoothly with them when they occur, even if they could not be predicted beforehand. The truth is that many kinds of difficulties cannot be anticipated. Most potentially stressful events, however, can be recognized easily and dealt with effectively when they come up. Looking at things this way is a constructive alternative to belief in the usefulness of worry. The person who chooses this alternative and understands its implications for daily functioning is very nearly invulnerable to anxieties. Her or his energy and attention will go into comfortable and intelligent planning for the future and dealing calmly with problems as they arise.

It is much easier to put mistaken beliefs into words than it is to articulate an alternative, calming outlook that might serve as a guide to stressfree living. Often, in life and psychotherapy, just gaining insight into the faulty assumptions that really determine one's outlook and feelings can bring tremendous relief and free energies for more relaxed and creative living. In many ways we think too much; we have too many beliefs and preconceptions about ourselves and the course of events. We might better eliminate many of them and live more spontaneously, being open to whatever happens and confident we can deal with any problems that arise. Nevertheless, we will try to put into words some of the positive principles involved in a worryfree outlook.

Someone who had gotten free of mistaken beliefs about the effectiveness of worry might say something like the following.

"I am aware that there are enormous uncertainties about the future. I do not know what next month's or next year's problems will turn out to be, let alone the solutions to them. Also, many disappointments and difficulties will arise that I can do absolutely nothing about, other than accept and turn my attention to other matters. Still, nothing prevents me from planning for the future, to the fullest extend possible, in a relaxed and unanxious manner. I can get the information I need to think things through and make my decisions fairly quickly in most cases. Then, until some new difficulty arises, there is nothing constructive to do except lose myself in the process of living, forget about past and future, live mostly in the present moment, and enjoy it! Serious planning and problem solving have nothing to do with worry about the future, and worrying about things I cannot change is equally useless and unproductive. I believe that it is possible to almost completely eliminate worry from my daily life."

Self-Worth and Performance Standards

Someone once wrote that the birthright of every American male is a chronic sense of personal inadequacy. The liberation of American women may mean that many will join their male counterparts in that nagging, chronic sense of "I'm not good enough" or "I'm not what I should be" that plagues so many individuals.

What is the source of this almost epidemic problem of fragile and lowered self-esteem? In large part the problem stems from the unrealistic expectations and unreachable standards we employ in judging our own behavior, and the fact that we make a connection between our basic self-worth as persons and others' evaluations of our social, professional, artistic, or athletic performances.

We all tend to take some standards and expectations of this kind for granted. A little reflection, however, makes it clear how natural and inevitable it is, given a belief in external standards of self-worth, that stress and anxiety will occur. Any linkage between self-esteem and performance standards immediately introduces great potential for feelings of danger and threat. Many different events can then indicate that we fall short of some established criterion. Those events will be perceived as threatening. The result is stress.

Tying one's self-worth to performance standards leads to excessive concern about other people's opinions. It results in fearful, alert looking to the reactions of others for clues as to where one stands in life or how one measures up in their eyes. Such concern, of course, is a sure recipe for stress. Other people often do not know what they really value or believe. Their standards and preferences are often inconsistent and therefore unattainable. Pleasing others, by itself, even when possible, is always a hollow victory. One may escape censure or disapproval. But one achieves nothing in terms of increased self-esteem. That can come only from pleasing yourself, which has nothing to do with external standards of self-worth.

When we set performance standards for ourselves that are unreachable, we labor under the curse of perfectionism. A perfectionist is someone who gets 99 percent on an exam and puts herself down for missing one question. A perfectionist is someone who focuses on the shortcomings and inadequacies of most things he does. He rarely compliments himself; he often criticizes himself. He is rarely pleased with the things he can do well, but often critical of himself for the things he cannot do well. For such a person, self-worth is continuously in jeopardy. Such a situation inevitably leads to perceptions of threat and to stress.

In a similar vein, Albert Ellis has suggested that one of the most common irrational beliefs that cause emotional disturbance is the belief that we must prove ourselves thoroughly adequate or competent in all, many, or at least some areas of living in order to feel worthwhile or secure. There are many idiosyncratic versions of this kind of belief. One may believe that "Everyone is basically equal and as good as anyone else, but in the real world you have a 'market value' that determines most of your happiness," or "Only highly talented or superior individuals can get the deepest kind of satisfaction out of their work." The variations are endless. And of course it is possible to believe many different, contradictory things. Perhaps most of us believe both that everyone is basically equal and that certain standards of value make some people more worthy than others.

It is important to realize how much of our inner life is involved in ongoing calculations, comparisons, and evaluations concerning our self-esteem. Ernest Becker has suggested that a great deal of our inner life, when we are not absorbed in some active task, is a "traffic in images of self-worth." We are continually saying things to ourselves like "I am good at that," "Look at what I accomplished here," "At least I'm not like that," "I can't do that very well," and so on. Much of this self-talk is an attempt to reaffirm a vital sense of inner worth. Much of it, unfortunately, is based on beliefs that link this sense of worth to standards of performance or the evaluations of other persons.

How can such beliefs be changed? It seems absolutely essential not to think in terms of replacing negative self-evaluations with positive ones. There is considerable danger in trying to replace self-criticism with something to the effect of "I do measure up," or even "I'm O.K." Rather, it seems to us that it is possible, and indeed necessary, to completely demolish the link between self-worth and any of our performances in any of life's roles. In practical terms this means something quite radical and unexpected. It means that one can learn to stop evaluating oneself at all, completely. Ultimately the only way to get rid of a problem behavior is to stop doing it. This notion applies equally to smoking, shoplifting, and thinking self-evaluative thoughts—thoughts that either affirm or undermine one's sense of self-worth by comparing one's qualities or behavior with standards of performance and the expectations of others.

It is very important to make a sharp distinction between evaluating what you do and evaluating what you are—between your actions and your self. There are judgments that are a necessary part of the fabric of everyday life. We regularly evaluate our experiences in terms of their pleasant, rewarding, or meaningful qualities. We evaluate our actions in terms of how effective or satisfying they are; whether they accomplish what they are intended to accomplish. But none of these evaluations necessarily involves anxiety or worry because none of them necessarily involves evaluating oneself, the person who does or experiences these things. Self-evaluation not only has a different focus—the person rather than his or her behavior—but uses different ideas or standards of evaluation, namely how worthwhile, important, or "good" the person really is. It is the process of evaluating oneself in this way, even positively, that eventually leads to stress.

The very idea of rating your "self," as if you were rating

physical beauty or assessing the firmness of tomatoes, makes little sense philosophically. Whether you picture the self as something behind one's behavior and experiences, a point at the center of them, or some elusive sense of identity that may change over time, it is difficult to get a clear fix on the object to be rated, and what sort of standards would be appropriate even if you could seems very obscure. This has lead some astute writers to conclude that almost all talk about the self and self-evaluation is literally nonsense. We are inclined to think that it is possible to talk meaningfully about self-esteem and some basis for it other than comparing oneself in a pseudo-objective way to standards and expectations. Such considerations, however, take us beyond our analysis of the psychology of stress, and we will discuss some of them briefly in a later chapter.

The pressing practical question is, "What would it be like to live without self-evaluations?" One can find beautiful statements that might be thought of as answers to this question in certain poems, the Sermon on the Mount, the writings of worldly mystics like Don Juan and Abraham Heschel, the sayings of Chuang Tzu, and elsewhere. These writings all seem to describe a kind of living that is relaxed, trusting, and self-forgetful. Living without self-evaluations is similar to engaging in task-oriented, as opposed to self-oriented, thinking. You might do nearly everything you did before, except now those doings are not regularly punctuated with self-evaluations. Or, you might do very different things because activities engaged in before out of fear, self-protection, or proving your worth now seems pointless and silly. It all depends on the individual case, although the principle remains the same.

It certainly is easier to put into words the mistaken beliefs that link self-worth and performance than it is to clearly articulate an alternative, stressfree outlook. Our stressful, self-defeating patterns of living are fairly similar and repetitive. But there are an uncountable number of different ways to express a personality that is not fettered by external standards of worth. Also, doing without such standards and expectations is better described as a process of living or way of getting involved with life than as a belief about it. Nevertheless, there appear to be some common denominators to the outlooks of individuals who have successfully broken the link between a sense of self-worth and outside factors. Such a person might say something like the following:

"I try to center my living around self-discovery rather than self-evaluation. I believe that it is always fruitless and leads to despair to be concerned with how successful or 'good' I am in other people's eyes. It is equally fruitless to become preoccupied with how I evaluate or judge myself, positively or negatively, by any standard. Not caring any longer about these expectations or standards means something very specific to me. It does not mean fighting them, but ignoring them. I do not pay any attention to them, but focus entirely on other things. When I can choose what I do, I avoid doing that for which my primary motive would be to avoid failure, achieve success, or establish my personal worth or importance.

"Instead, I believe it is always fruitful to sort of 'forget' myself and get involved in things that are intrinsically rewarding or meaningful, out of such motives as curiosity, mastery, love, or pleasure. The result always is that I discover new facets of myself and enrich my experience of myself and the world. This brings with it a deeper and more solid sense of myself, and creates a feeling of self-acceptance that has nothing to do with external standards of worth. The path of self-discovery precludes such standards and expectations because you do not know in advance what your experience will be like. Therefore, you cannot steer it in the 'right' direction. By the time you do know, you already possess something much more valuable than self-evaluative thinking can ever provide. Living this way does not preclude uncertainty, risk, disappointment, or tragedy. But it can virtually eliminate anxiety and threat concerning a sense of personal worth."

The Locus of Emotional Security

One of the major concerns people have is how secure or insecure they feel about their relationships with people who are emotionally important to them. A great deal of anxiety is experienced within intimate love relationships. Many Americans are enormously preoccupied with love and sex and chronically anxious about them.

Emotional security refers simply to the degree that you believe you can find, develop, maintain, and enjoy emotionally important relationships. Mistaken beliefs concerning emotional security all have in common the fact that they place that security in, or link it to, someone or something outside oneself. It may be a spouse or lover, a circle of friends, persons in one's family or among in-laws, customers, bosses, or others. Beliefs falling in this category may vary widely, from "My standing with my professional peers means everything to me," to "The most devastating thing that could happen to me would be to lose my wife's (or husband's) love and emotional support." All of these beliefs involve, to one degree or another, locating one's emotional security or anchor outside oneself.

Emotionally close and comfortable relationships with other persons are important to virtually everyone. Some of the characteristics of such relationships are feelings of warmth and affection, honesty and mutual trust, a sense of being known and liked as a unique individual, spontaneity, comfortableness about being your unguarded real self, and an easy and gratifying exchange of ideas and viewpoints. Mutual liking, good communication, and spontaneity provide us with some of our deepest gratifications in living.

However, it is always a mistake to tie one's sense of security or confidence about being able to obtain these deeply pleasurable and gratifying experiences to specific people or forces outside oneself. To rely or depend upon any other particular person or situation for the possibility of emotionally rewarding relationships, even to a small degree, is to put yourself under stress. The complexity of persons, the likelihood that they (even those closest to us) will grow or change in unpredictable ways, and the ever-present possibility of outside events interfering with or disrupting our relationships make us decidedly vulnerable—if we locate any of our emotional security outside ourselves.

One of the authors recently had several hundred individuals fill out a newly developed Social Anxiety Inventory that listed over 150 everyday social situations, such as "striking up a conversation with a stranger on a bus or plane" and "telling a friend you are angry with him about some incident," that are not in fact dangerous, but are perceived as threatening by many people. They were asked to rate on a five-point scale, from "not at all" to "very much," how much fear or anxiety they usually experience in these situations. The item that received the highest average rating (most anxiety) was "thoughts of losing a girlfriend/boyfriend or spouse." Why are we so afraid of losing our intimate relationships?

Love relationships and close friendships provide us with deeply fulfilling and gratifying experiences. But the rewarding quality of these relationships, by itself, does not explain why we fear losing them to the extent we do. There is no simple explanation. But one important factor seems to be that many people mistakenly believe that if they lose an important relationship they will not be able to find another person who means as much to them. They commonly think their happiness depends upon the continuation of the present relationship. These beliefs are entirely false. In the worst case, loss of a relationship says nothing about one's future prospects. Usually, of course, the fact that you currently have a good relationship indicates that future opportunities are likely to present themselves, and that you have the skills to take advantage of them when they do.

Certainly it appears that we often intentionally distort our image of the future and its prospects for rewarding relationships. We may do so in order to justify clinging to present relationships, to make others feel guilty about leaving us, or to escape some of the risks and loneliness that, for better or worse, are a part of everyone's life. Nevertheless, the mistaken belief that loss of a relationship bodes ill for the future is a major source of emotional insecurity and stress.

Doing entirely without emotional security that is anchored in other people or outside situations really means replacing that kind of security with a sense of confidence in oneself to create and enjoy emotionally rewarding relationships whenever that is desired and possible. Usually the less confidence one has in one's abilities to create such relationships, the more one seeks to anchor one's emotional security in outside factors.

Mistaken beliefs about the locus of emotional security result in two common patterns of coping with other people who are emotionally important to us. One of these patterns involves allowing closeness and attachment to another person, but then coming to depend excessively upon that individual.

Many people get married, make friends, or have children, in part because they believe that the other person in this relationship will provide some quality they lack that will make them feel more self-confident or worthy as individuals. They are always disappointed. No relationship can provide a basis for self-confidence or self-esteem. One always ends up blaming, resenting, even hating the other person or persons in this kind of relationship. The disappointment is a bitter one, and many relationships do not survive it.

Other individuals distance themselves emotionally from other people and never form close, rewarding relationships. They may allow private feelings of affection to develop for others, and even suspect that they are reciprocated. But rarely are these feelings disclosed to the other person. The risk of rejection is too great. They remain isolated and alone.

Both overdependency on others and isolation from them can stem from the same type of mistaken belief. Usually people are afraid of losing a close relationship for the same reason they are afraid of forming one in the first place—because they locate their emotional security outside themselves. The alternative, locating your emotional security entirely within yourself, does not tend to lessen or limit your involvement with others. It enhances mutually rewarding involvements. It leads you to feel much more relaxed about the prospect of initiating or deepening relationships, and greatly lessens your tendency to cling to relationships that are no longer fulfilling. Undoing mistaken beliefs about emotional security, however, might mean for many people that they would choose to spend more time alone, be comfortable in their solitude, and find creative or fulfilling things to do with aloneness or solitude that would deepen and enrich their lives.

Correcting mistaken beliefs about emotional security requires that we acknowledge that each of us is very much alone and on his own in the world. Recognizing this fact does not prevent realizing any realistic potential for emotionally rewarding relationships, including lifelong friendships and marriage. In fact, such a recognition enhances this potential. Self-confidence, initiative, and willingness to take risks in creating such relationships must come from within. No one else can make you a confident, secure person. Most of us accept this principle to some degree, but we usually exempt from it a few relationships or security ties, and secretly rely on them for emotional security. Someone's approval, love, or understanding serves as an emotional hedge against uncertainty and change.

There is certainly nothing morally wrong with investing a portion of one's emotional security in outside people or situations. If anything, it is normal to do so in this society, and unless taken to extremes, it does not lead to serious emotional problems. However, it inevitably does produce stress. Every event that signals potential or actual change in these relationships will give rise to perceptions of threat, even if only to a small degree. It may not be possible to undo the stress many of us put ourselves under without first undoing the link between emotional security and specific relationships. Only then can we relax and enjoy ourselves completely in these relationships, and also be able at other times to turn our attention completely away from them, so that worries about our emotional investments do not interfere with other activities.

The outlook of someone whose locus of emotional security was within himself might be expressed in the following words.

"People are important to me. I highly value my intimate relationships. I am a human, a social animal, and need people in order to fully express certain aspects of my humanness. But no relationship can make me feel secure in the world if I am not secure within myself. Changes in any of my important relationships might sadden or disappoint me. Fate could deal me some cruel blows. But the world is full of people. Among those people there are some I could care for and who would care for me. I am not dependent on one person or group of persons for my happiness."

Perceived Inferiority or Disadvantage

The final category of anxiety-producing beliefs has to do with perceived inferiority or disadvantage. Very often people believe that they are inferior to other people, or that they have some basic disadvantage as compared with other people in our common struggle to lead some kind of stable and satisfying life. They may perceive themselves to be inferior. Or they may perceive their personalities or situations in life to be permanently disadvantaged in some important respect.

Perceived inferiority is the belief that there is some deficit in yourself or your background that makes it difficult for you to lead a satisfying life. Obviously, by any standard one cares to select, we are all inferior to many people and superior to some others. It is virtually impossible to be the best or worst at anything. Most of us, of course, present a very mixed picture of talents and accomplishments. We also come from very different kinds of backgrounds, face very different kinds of obstacles in pursuit of our goals, and have widely varying degrees of luck. These are hard facts of life that cannot be denied. But ability, wealth, beauty, and accomplishments do not guarantee a sense of self-confidence. Feelings of inferiority are quite widespread among the very people who seem to have the most going for them in their lives. Often these people combine a belief in external standards of self-worth with perfectionism. Dissolving the connection between self-worth and external standards can do much to help such people lead more satisfying lives. However, overcoming a basic sense of being handicapped and forever frustrated in the pursuit of happiness often requires a certain understanding of, and attitude toward, the human situation. It is most helpful to carry with us a deep sense of being part of the human race and sharing in the common human struggle. Perhaps the most important part of this sense of shared humanity is a deep feeling of fundamental equality with other human beings, all of them. There is a tragic dimension to human life that overshadows other differences among us and makes us basically equal. Everyone suffers deep disappointments, watches many of their hopes and ambitions go up in smoke, painfully sheds many illusions, lives with uncertainty, and sooner or later faces death. Any wisdom that can be gleaned from our struggle is available to us all.

No realist would claim that human life is generally a happy thing. However, there are moments, sometimes longer stretches of time, when we enjoy deeply pleasurable and meaningful experiences. At least some of these experiences are available to everyone, and it is not the number or quantity of them that matters. Just a few of them can provide a person with a certain qualitative sense of life that is difficult to describe. It is a feeling of solidness or realness, a sense of really being alive and, later, of really having lived or been a part of whatever it is that human life is all about. Because of shared experiences of tragedy and equal access to this basic experience of being part of the human drama, it is possible for every person to feel entirely worthwhile and important as anyone else and on an equal footing with every other member of the race.

Many people, however, do not feel fundamentally equal to all other human beings. They perceive themselves as lacking or inferior in some way that handicaps them in the pursuit of a satisfying life and robs them of their basic dignity as persons. It is difficult to define this inferiority because it is not a rational concept. Sometimes it is perceived as a lack in oneself of some kind of charm or likability or ability to make an impact on other people. Sometimes it is perceived as something more concrete, as a lack of intelligence, good looks, stamina, or any of a dozen other "good" qualities. Sometimes it is externalized and perceived more as disadvantage than inferiority, as a lack of background, education, social status, money, or "connections" that block the pursuit of satisfying goals in living. Often the sense of inferiority is vague and undefined, although one may see it reflected in inner dissatisfaction or outward failure to achieve one's goals.

Often, perceived inferiority emerges clearly in the form of mistaken beliefs about how one stacks up against other people in terms of coping with everyday problems and stresses. Such beliefs are variations of the theme that "some other people lead smooth and almost painless lives and there must be something wrong with me because I don't." One may mistakenly perceive that at least some other people do not experience the stresses, uncertainties, and self-doubts that one does oneself. Or, one may incorrectly perceive that some other people possess some kind of magic coping skill that makes their experience of these stresses less painful or difficult than one's own. There is good evidence that one of the chief benefits of successful group therapy is its effectiveness in bringing home unmistakably to participants the fact that people (including therapists) are far more alike than different, and that they experience very much the same kinds of struggles and doubts in living. This awareness tends to dissolve perceptions of inferiority. It also can help to make it clear that changing one's thinking about stressful situations (the best way to reduce stress) is equally possible for everyone.

There are two ways people commonly respond to perceptions of inferiority or disadvantage and the stress they create. They may strive to overcome disadvantage or compensate for inferiority by running faster to catch up—by extra effort, adding to their strengths, piling up additional accomplishments where possible. Or, they associate with people they believe to be stronger or better than they are, in the hope that they will offer protection or somehow make up for basic deficiencies. But strategies of compensation through extra effort or dependency on others never really work. We come to resent the extra effort that is required of us but not of others, and we eventually feel hostile toward those depended upon to supply something lacking in ourselves.

In addition, strategies of compensation do not accomplish their goal of actually making up for some original lack or inferiority. If anything, the gulf usually widens. It gradually becomes clear that no amount of compensatory effort or accomplishment can purchase a sense of basic equality with all other persons, any more than external accomplishments by themselves can provide a sense of basic self-worth. You can exert yourself or rely on others, but the bitter awareness grows that the payoff will never come. Nothing can compensate for perceived inferiorities. They sap your energies and rob you of the motivation to achieve in healthy ways. They discourage, and the discouragement tends to grow.

The first step in undoing perceived inferiorities is to become aware that they exist and aware of the self-defeating strategies of compensation that may have grown up around them. The next step is easy enough to describe, although it is not possible to give a certain recipe for how to take it or a sure guide for coping with the anguish that may be involved. You must decide that you are not inferior but are fundamentally equal to every other human being, and that nothing but your own mistaken beliefs stands between yourself and a full share, full ownership rights, and full participation in the common human struggle. Then you must begin to act as if this were really the case, and see what happens. Some of the chapters in Part 2 of this book present some guidelines for this kind of action.

A psychological perspective on stress can make clear the essential connection between mistaken beliefs, such as external standards of self-worth, and everyday stress and anxiety. Also, this kind of psychological analysis of the problem can be an essential tool in learning to cope more effectively with stress. However, it seems likely that for many persons the battle with stress will have to involve the development of a positive personal philosophy that commits them to a certain view of their relations to the universe and the meaning of their participation in the shared human struggle. Such a personal philosophy may be indispensable in cultivating a stronge sense of self-worth and fundamental equality with others. A psychological analysis of the stress problem can, in our opinion, open up the question of philosophical commitment in new and exciting ways. But the actual crafting of such a personal philosophy takes us beyond a purely psychological approach to the problem of stress. We will briefly discuss some of these issues in the next chapter.

part 2

coping
with stress

6

notes toward a
stressfree
philosophy
of living

We have stated that stress lies in the perception of events, not in events themselves. Perceiving events as threatening to our egos or thwarting of our efforts leads to harmful emotional arousal. This is the problem of stress—not outside situations or other persons, but our ideas about them and what they mean to us. Most of the ideas that produce stress can be boiled down to a few key mistaken beliefs about ourselves and the world. These beliefs are emotionally charged and highly evaluative. They lead us to make cruel and impossible demands upon ourselves and others. They are the root cause of the hurry, frustration, and growing sense of hopelessness that often characterize overstressed lives. In this chapter and the one that follows we will address the topic of recognizing and changing stress-producing beliefs.

Before discussing how to change beliefs it may be useful to

review briefly what we are trying to change *from*, and to catch a glimpse of the kind of outlook we might be trying to change *to*. The problem of stress, in large measure, is a philosophical problem, a problem of beliefs. It is not a matter of uncontrollable fight-or-flight reflexes, or some kind of mass contemporary neurosis. It is a matter of lacking a constructive philosophy of living. Psychology cannot by itself provide the positive beliefs and values to live by for which we are all searching. But it can raise the question of values afresh in some exciting and useful ways. The right kind of psychological analysis of the stress problem can, perhaps, go even a bit further and cast a few solid beams of light into the darkness. It can identify some of the necessary ingredients of *any* philosophy of living that would be able to minimize stress in today's world. You can see if you think this is true as we go along.

Prescription for Stress

Remember that the stress reaction is triggered by perceptions of threat to our emotional security or self-esteem, or by perceptions of others' wrongful interference with our lives. Usually these perceptions are distorted in ways we have discussed. Faulty perceptions are rooted in faulty beliefs. The perceptions will not change until there is a change in underlying belief. Mistaken beliefs that produce anger and anxiety are a sure prescription for stress. They structure our view of the world and our patterns of daily living so that chronic tension, arousal, and stress are inevitable.

At this point you may find it helpful to recall the main kinds of anxiety and anger-producing perceptions and beliefs discussed in earlier chapters. We have claimed that there are certain styles of thinking and living that are likely to predispose us to harmful, fatiguing emotional arousal. They are:

1. Holding superstitious beliefs that worry prevents mistakes and misfortune, helps anticipate the future, or gives you added control over the course of events.
2. Evaluating yourself as less worthy or deserving a person because you fall short of some standard of performance or expectation of others.
3. Believing that your emotional security and the pros-

74

pect of rewarding relationships are tied to specific people and situations upon which you depend for affection and love.

4. Regarding yourself as inferior or permanently disadvantaged as compared with some other people, making it difficult or impossible for you to lead a satisfying life.

5. Having extensive personal boundaries, overidentification with too many people, things, and ideas, so that you are vulnerable to irritation and threat in too many areas.

6. Adopting a competitive, win-lose orientation that makes living into a series of contests, and tends to put your self-esteem on the line in every life situation.

7. Engaging in moralistic thinking about how others should and should not behave that leads to feelings of anger, frustration, and moral indignation.

8. Attributing the negative or disappointing behavior of other people to their enduring intentions or basic personality traits, leading to condemnation of others, anger, and intolerance.

9. Believing that you have a right to be free from discomfort or deserve to get what you want, which produces a low tolerance for life's inevitable frustrations.

Just gaining insight into mistaken beliefs and their emotional consequences can bring a sense of relief and a positive change in attitude. New beliefs can evolve spontaneously once old ones have been raised to awareness and effectively questioned. But it is best not to leave the development of a positive outlook to chance. Most of us have been indoctrinated in a great deal of erroneous thinking concerning the sources of emotional arousal. The major obstacles to belief change are faulty assumptions to which we are often unaware. Many of these faulty assumptions have in common the fact that they blind us to the uncertainty, limitations, and precariousness that are inherent in human existence. We need to clarify and examine some of these assumptions before turning to the topic of positive beliefs.

Human Limitations

Part of the continuing tension of overstressed lives seems to be a direct result of our lack of a consistent, positive belief system to live by. Sometimes we sense directly that this is true. We sense that there is a gap between the conventional wisdom that guides our daily activities and some deeper wisdom about things. We try to be optimistic, do what is right, and keep on scurrying to get somewhere. But there are a lot of nagging doubts about whether we can really deal effectively with the challenges we face. A solid sense of being in touch with deeper currents of reality seems to elude us. Because of this gap, this lack of solid footing, we sometimes feel apprehensive and vulnerable. From time to time a disappointment will pull the rug out from under, leaving us feeling painfully helpless and lost.

The great Italian novelist, Ignazio Silone, wrote:

> Every mask and every pretense can be reduced to one great evasion: the desire to overcome the sorrows of life with palliatives and tricks of the imagination rather than with sincerity and impulsion. . . . But there is a sorrow inherent in our human fate, which we must learn how to face and make into our friend.

To a degree all mistaken, stress-producing beliefs are rooted in an outlook that encourages us to avoid directly facing and coming to terms with the sorrows and limitations of human life. This outlook holds out the promise of having our self-esteem, emotional security, and sense of moral rightness securely grounded in something outside ourselves. Then we would be like lucky children, borrowing much-needed strength and approval from reliable powers greater than ourselves. That, of course, would be an illusion. There are no such powers that will take care of us or do our thinking for us. We have to decide for ourselves what life is all about in an uncertain world. Part of the tension and drivenness we experience comes from a continuing effort to pretend that things are different from the way they really are.

Miriam described herself as a "creative housewife." She married Hal during her junior year at college. While he pursued a successful career as a petroleum engineer and served two terms on their city council and four years as president of the local board of education, she spent twenty-five years diligently carrying out her part of the family enterprise. She took care of the monthly bills, kept the house clean and in good repair, cooked for her family, and entertained regularly for their friends and for business associates of her husband. She was blessed with a sturdy and optimistic nature that carried her through periods of fatigue and self-doubt when, as she might confide in a friend, she felt "more used than appreciated." She had, in fact, more political acumen and public-speaking ability than her husband, but devoted her energies to his campaigns for public office. Much of her life was spent ferrying three children back and forth from home to schools, lessons, soccer practice, and summer camp. She worked hard to provide them with opportunities to develop their talents, stressed the values of achievement and self-discipline, but tried to emphasize other values of love and unselfishness as well.

Within the space of two years during Miriam's middle forties everything seemed to come apart. Miriam and Hal's oldest son, their "golden child" whose good looks, many talents, and self-confidence filled them with pride and happiness, was tragically killed in an automobile accident. Their younger son, who had always seemed to live in his older brother's shadow and was shy and moody despite his parents' efforts to encourage him, reacted very badly to the accident. During the year following the accident he became progressively more involved in drugs and eventually dropped out of high school. One evening a month later his parents found a letter telling them that he had quit drugs, joined a religious sect that believed in living apart from the world, moved to a communal farm in a South American country, and did not wish to communicate with his parents again. Very shortly thereafter Hal told Miriam that he was leaving her for a younger woman with whom he had been having an affair. His last words to her after an incredibly painful conversation about his plans were: "I will always love you. I know what I'm doing is probably wrong and I may just make a fool out of myself. But after what has happened to my sons life just doesn't have much meaning any more. This relationship is exciting and makes me feel really alive at times—I just have to see where it takes me."

Charles astounded his family and friends by turning down several promising offers of positions with large corporations when he graduated from college. Instead he went to work for a small, floundering construction business that he felt had excellent long-term prospects for someone with his entrepreneurial skills. He soon took over the company and worked twelve hours a day for fifteen years, occasionally taking a Sunday off. He liked to describe himself to friends as "the most relaxed workaholic I ever knew." Indeed, he enjoyed his work and poured himself into it. His income began to rise as the company first turned a profit and then became highly successful. He seized an opportunity to "make it big" one year by turning down some business to prepare for work on two large federally funded projects in his part of the state. He felt certain he would win the contract for these projects. But at the last minute he was underbid by a much larger company that had political connections and could afford to take a loss in order to expand its operations. As a consequence he was forced to sell out to this very company in order to avoid bankruptcy.

Charles realized a substantial profit from the sale of his company. But he had no other savings, and no plans for the future. He felt devastated and lost. Forced to reexamine his life, he looked around and discovered that his two children, who were close to leaving home, were complete strangers to him. They only resented his attempts to communicate with them now, after years of neglect. He found also that he had not really talked with his wife in years, which helped explain why there was no affection between them any longer, and why sex was now impossible. He endured his pain about all this, alone and depressed, for a period of four months. Then he suffered a serious heart attack.

"Miriam" and "Charles" are stereotypes, of course. But there is at least a little of them in most of us. They were uncommonly decent, hardworking individuals who put forth their best effort. They played by the rules. They endured much stress and inconvenience without complaint, and made few excuses for themselves when the going got rough. By any reasonable standard they worked not only hard but skillfully at trying to reach their goals of happiness and success for themselves and their families. What went wrong?

Some simple truths about the human condition escaped these sincere, hardworking individuals. They believed that through their efforts they could guarantee a successful and happy future. Therefore they aimed their lives toward the future, struggling and sacrificing to reach that better day we all dream of. They seemed to repress the knowledge that their plans could be smashed at any time by accident or misfortune. It seemed to them very likely that they would reach their goals. They seemed to believe that they could predict the future—that life would deal them no unexpected blows. They did not realize the extent of our human limitations. They did not acknowledge how precarious and uncertain life really is, and how limited is our ability to anticipate and control future events. They failed to see clearly that they could not avoid the pain and tragedy that, in some form, are inevitably a part of every human life.

The greatest tragedy of these lives, however, was that—believing the future was under their control—they put off many kinds of satisfaction and joy in living until a later time that never arrived. They failed to savor life as it was lived, to smell the flowers as they walked along. They turned down opportunities to engage in many intrinsically satisfying and pleasurable activities because they were not instrumental in achieving future goals. They consequently did not develop their abilities, interpersonal relationships, and personal philosophies so as to have enabled them to better withstand the inevitable hardships of life. Instead they concentrated on trying to reach happiness in the future. Of course, the future never quite works out the way we think it will.

Most who adopt this kind of unthinking, future-oriented style of living have one thing in common. They lack a philosophy of living that helps them accept human limitations and live creatively within them. They lack an orientation toward life that gives them a clear picture of how they can involve themselves in a meaningful, harmonious way in a life that is highly precarious, uncertain, and bounded by death and the unknown. As are most of us, they are true believers in the contemporary myths of Progress and Happiness.

Some Contemporary Myths

Our conventional wisdom about living in twentieth-century America does not help us face up to our limitations, our lack of control over our destiny. Our official public philosophy of life rests upon the twin pillars of the myth of Progress and the myth of Happiness, which purport to tell us what life is all about. No schoolchild fails to get the message that his or her destiny is to be as happy and successful as possible in the context of a society that is making steady technological and political progress. We are forward-looking and happiness-oriented. The myths of Progress and Happiness run together. Our individual success is thought to contribute to economic and social progress, and our attainment of happiness is proof positive that more and more of the "good life" is being realized. These popular myths are, in their own way, a prescription for stress because they ignore the limitations and ambiguity of human life. They set impossible, even ridiculous standards for individual and collective achievement. They produce the chronic arousal, tension, and stress that always accompany measuring yourself against external standards of worthiness and trying, through effort and worry, to make the future turn out the way it should.

Standards of Progress, in the sense of some general movement of history or human affairs, are presumptuous and unprovable. Michael Novak has written

It seems indispensable to a technological society like ours to be future-oriented, forward-looking, fascinated by hope. The illusion of progress is the prop that takes the place of God; many cling to it. Could Americans endure life without ever new frontiers? . . . Suppose the American myth of progress, pragmatism, and fulfillment is wrong. Suppose the human costs of progress, for which we have no measure, are steeper than the technical gains we are so fond of measuring.

In line with the myth of Progress we are fond of thinking that our science and technology eventually can produce an answer to every question we might ask, and train for us an expert with a straightforward solution to every problem we face. Again, we lack a sense of limits. Our cultural outlook emphasizes expanding human possibilities. We are committed to maximizing individual rights and fulfillment, with a special emphasis on scientific technology as a means for controlling the environment in order to meet basic survival needs, minimize pain and disease, and provide the material abundance and leisure time necessary for the pursuit of other goals. It seems desirable to expand human possibilities, even to maximize them. But we clearly have bitten off more than we can chew or digest properly. We are overwhelmed and have become quite strung out with a sense of almost infinite possibilities. There seem to be so many different possible life styles, pleasures, relationships, careers, experiences and even values to be tried on for size.

Having limitless choices and possibilities (or thinking one does) really means having very few. There is no basis for choice or wisdom to guide the process of choosing. Thus we begin to lose control of our living. We take on more than we can handle in the present. We more and more fantasize about and live in the future as the place where more can be accomplished and enjoyed. It is not clear, however, what we really want. Therefore means get substituted for ends (all in the name of progress). Technology, achievement, power and control, material security and possessions become ends in themselves rather than means for reaching some (certainly not all) desirable states of living. We get involved in increasingly frantic activity that is often accompanied by an increasing sense of meaninglessness about where it is all headed.

The myth of Progress is really a counsel of despair. It depreciates the past and present and exalts the future. There is no reason to believe that ancient Chinese sages or Greek philosophers or uncountable numbers of ordinary men and women through the ages necessarily achieved less wisdom or experienced less of what it means to be human than ourselves. Instead of locating ourselves somewhere along a straight line of progress extending into the indefinite future, we might better think of ourselves as traveling around a circle of self-discovery and human destiny that has been followed by many in the past and will be followed by others again. The line of Progress is depersonalizing and externalizes our sense of worth. It forces us to think of ourselves evaluatively and comparatively, in terms of more or less, better or worse. It instills greed and desperation. We must refuse to see ourselves as instruments or conduits of Progress, as means to the end of the future or a humanity that is better or better off than ourselves. The only way to do this may be to see ourselves as one with the human travelers of past and future generations. We may act out our shared destiny in different ways, using different words and symbols, but in the last analysis it is the same circle of discovery. The more things change, the more they remain the same.

The myth of Happiness, also, is not a very happy myth. It is astounding to see what a psychological burden the idea of happiness can become. Many people actually feel guilty because they are not happy in general or at some particular time. They seem to feel that not being happy reflects negatively on their accomplishments or worth as a person, and think less of themselves as a result. The burden gets spread around. Parents feel guilty if their children are not happy, and children feel they have let their parents down if their lives are not ruled by joy and contentment. Excessive concern about making one's friend, lover, or spouse happy contributes to the ruin of many intimate relationships. Obviously the idea of happiness, one's own or someone else's, has become yet another standard against which we measure our personal worth, thereby producing stress.

Part of the problem stems from the vague and contradictory meanings we attach to the concept of happiness. In one of its meanings the idea of happiness is a negative concept. It implies that happiness is the absence of pain, dissatisfaction, or despair. It tells you what to avoid, not what to seek. This notion of happiness is a very poor guide to living. First of all, a certain amount of emotional pain, many disappointments and dissatisfactions, and some despair are an inevitable part of life. Their occurrence is generally unpredictable, but occur they will. The pursuit of happiness, therefore, can easily become a process of seeking to avoid the unavoidable and blaming yourself when you fail to avoid it, making yourself even more unhappy.

Happiness can be defined positively as a psychological state of contentment, fulfillment, or peace of mind. Our everyday notion of happiness as a goal in living is probably a mixture of the negative and positive definitions of it. Happiness as a positive goal also breeds stress. Because it is a goal it leads to worrying about the future, worrying about losing happiness if you have it, and finding it if you do not.

When happiness is a goal you may find that you are saying to yourself, "How happy am I? Other people seem to be happier than I am (I have failed somehow). Why am I so unhappy? What have I done wrong? Whose fault is it? Could I have done differently? How?" Striving for happiness leads to self-preoccupation and self-evaluation. Persons preoccupied with their happiness are rarely happy.

Happiness cannot be achieved when it is pursued directly as a goal in living. Efforts to capture happiness, nail it down, or make it a secure possession always either spoil it or miss it completely. Happiness is any form is a transitory experience, not some final state at which we arrive. Much of what is pleasurable about happy moments is their spontaneous and unexpected character. Permanent contentment, even if we could achieve it, would lead quickly to boredom and restlessness.

The myth of Happiness, like much advertising and many popular television shows, treats us more like objects to be manipulated than the interesting persons we really are. It conveys an image of us as one part worried workaholic and one part mindless little kitten that needs only a tummy full of warm milk (new car, improved laundry soap, social success) in order to be happy. It suggests that happiness can be obtained (even purchased) directly, made permanent, and that there is something wrong with us if this is not accomplished. The idea of happiness as a goal in living or a final state we arrive at leads to chronic disappointment, self-criticism, and stress. It distracts us mightily from the things we can do to minimize stressful emotions and get on with living.

Stress-producing beliefs all involve illusions and a certain measure of self-deception about the human condition. Trying to divine the future through worrying, restlessly extending personal boundaries in the search for accomplishment, suppressing fatigue and neglecting the needs of the body, twisting and turning to be good in the eyes of others who are basically as uncertain as oneself, trying to find emotional security (or even the meaning of life) in the love of another person, and chronic irritation at people and events that "get in the way" all involve an element of trying to ignore or deny our human limitations. They may or may not involve belittling others or trying to get power over their lives. But within the sphere of our own living they do involve trying to get more control over the course of events, sometimes including other people, than really is possible.

The contemporary myths of Progress and Happiness help perpetuate a distorted view of the human situation. They emphasize certain possibilities of human living and downplay its limitations. They encourage us to respond to the limits of life with increased effort and positive thinking, whether or not they make any real difference in the quality of our lives. Thus they contribute to the problem of stress. They lead us to do more, try harder, and criticize ourselves (instead of our faulty beliefs) if the results of continued striving do not add to our sense of self-esteem and pleasure in living.

Guidelines for a Low-Stress Life Style

Relief from stress and the beginning of wisdom come when we stop denying the basic uncertainty of life and our lack of control over many of its outcomes. Then we can step back and contemplate both our remarkable possibilities and our awesome limitations, without emphasizing one side of the picture at the expense of the other. We can keep both limitations and possibilities in full view as we make important choices and commitments. Living this way may demand a sometimes painful shedding of illusions, a great deal of maturity, creative risk taking, and the elimination of many comforting excuses and rationalizations. The rewards of this approach, however, can be very substantial. They may include the deep pleasure of self-acceptance and a certain invulnerability to the nagging self-doubts and chronic tension of stressful living.

What follows is our attempt to state some basic positive beliefs and guidelines for living to the fullest while avoiding much of the stress of life that is epidemic in today's world. These positive beliefs certainly do not make up a complete philosophy of life. They or something like them, however, may form a necessary part of a stressfree outlook. The quotations from varied times and authors that accompany these statements of belief should help to bring home the point that while there may be renewed understanding, there is little under the sun that is really new.

Guideline 1

> *The mind is its own place, and in itself*
> *Can make a heaven of hell, a hell of heaven.*
> —John Milton

Men are not worried by things, but by their ideas about things. When we meet with difficulties, become enxious or troubled, let us not blame others, but rather ourselves, that is, our ideas about things.

—Epictetus

I saw that all the things I feared, and which feared me, had nothing good or bad in them save insofar as the mind was affected by them.

—Spinoza

If you are pained by an external thing, it is not this thing that disturbs you, but your own judgment about it. And it is in your power to wipe out this judgment now.

—Marcus Aurelius

We are influenced not by "facts" but by our interpretation of facts.

—Alfred Adler

> *There is nothing either good or bad,*
> *But thinking makes it so.*
> —Shakespeare

It is not what happens to us, but our perceptions, beliefs, and what we tell ourselves about what happens to us that produce stressful emotions, and cause almost all forms of emotional distress.

As we have pointed out many times, it is our perceptions, our view of the world, that create stress, not the world itself. For the most part we are the authors of our tragedy and pathos. In a real sense we manufacture most of the dramas that we act out in life. To begin to free oneself from stress is to ask oneself the question "How much can this thing I am worried or angry about affect me apart from the meaning I attach to it?" Few things are really "terrible," "dreadful," "horrible," "disastrous," "awful," "disgusting," "disgraceful," "humiliating," or "abhorrent." Yet we often use these or synonymous terms to characterize our reactions to events. We react to fundamentally minor problems as though they were major catastrophes. This is largely because our belief systems have caused us to attach great significance to minor happenings. It is within our power to adopt beliefs that lead to illness and emotional suffering. But so too can we choose beliefs and patterns of living that lead to serenity and health.

Guideline 2
The virtue lies in the struggle, not the prize.
—Lord Houghton

Happiness cannot be achieved when pursued as a goal. Happiness is never sought and achieved directly. It is always a byproduct of other activities. The expression "the pursuit of happiness" is a contradiction in terms. Pursuing happiness leads to worry over how happy we are and, hence, to stress and self-preoccupation. Self-preoccupied people are rarely happy. Happiness usually results from an ability to stop focusing on yourself and become absorbed in other activities.

Guideline 3
Wherefore I perceive that there is nothing better, than that a man should rejoice in his own works; for that is his portion . . .
—Ecclesiastes 3:22

Find activities from which you derive *intrinsic* satisfaction. Stressful emotions can be reduced by focusing on the process

86

or style of your activities, rather than on their results or outcomes. Do those things which enable you to focus on and enjoy the activity itself, rather than focus on how well you are performing or what the activity will bring you.

Guideline 4

Man finds himself by finding his place, and he finds his place by finding appropriate others that need his care and that he needs to care for. Through caring and being cared for man experiences himself as part of nature; we are closest to a person or an idea when we help it grow.
—Milton Mayeroff

Find something other than yourself and your achievements to care about and believe in. A sense of purpose and meaning comes from dedication to a person, a relationship, an idea, or set of values. This sense of purpose can be a kind of existential compass that can guide you through the storms of stressful living.

Guideline 5

What is life?
I do not know.
—Poem by a four-year-old child

Learn to recognize and accept both your personal shortcomings and your lack of control over much of what will ultimately happen to you. For some people it is acceptance of the permanent uncertainty and ambiguity of life that finally cuts the knots of senseless striving, or allows them to give up the burden of pretending to be more "in the know" than anyone else. As a middle-aged client of ours, who had finally quit domineering his wife and children after many years, remarked, "It is very hard to be right all the time, especially when you usually don't know what you are talking about."

Guideline 6

Men have been wise in very different modes; but they have always laughed in the same way.
—Samuel Johnson

Develop an unhostile, benevolent sense of humor. Most people believe they already possess a good sense of humor. Few really do.

As Max Beerbohm noted, much of what we call humor involves either "delight in suffering" or "contempt for the unfamiliar." Although much humor possesses a hostile quality, there is a kind of delightful laughter that springs from a sense of the comedy and absurdity of life. Learning to laugh at oneself not only brings relief from tension, it also facilitates self-acceptance.

Guideline 7

To err is human, to forgive divine.
—Alexander Pope

Learn to tolerate and forgive both yourself and others. To use Albert Ellis' expression, we are all "fallible human beings." Intolerance of our own frailities leads to stress, tension, and low self-esteem. Intolerance of others leads to blame and anger.

We do not have godlike powers to legislate the right and wrong of human conduct. Part of being human is pursuing "the good" as we see it. But we have no solid grounds for expecting others to follow the particular values we follow at the moment. Stop imposing your values on others. Live and let live.

Guideline 8

We must have the gift to identify ourselves with other persons, to relive their experience and to feel its conflicts as our own . . . in order that we shall feel in their lives what we know in our own; the human dilemma.
—J. Bronowski

Learn to see the world and yourself through the eyes of others. Our interpersonal relationships are less stressful and unhappy when we understand the viewpoints of others. Empathy is an antidote to blame and anger.

Guideline 9

Other people are not in this world to live up to your expectations.

—Fritz Perls

We are, each of us, the protagonists of our personal plays. We all need some things from others but we must take ultimate responsibility for our own happiness. No other person can make you happy and secure. You must do this for yourself.

Guideline 10
Flowers won't grow in a weed patch.
—Saying

A low-stress life style typically is reasonably efficient and well-managed. Laziness, self-indulgence, and sloppiness usually create more stress than they remove.

Guideline 11
When you get there, there isn't any there there.
—Gertrude Stein

The struggles of life change; they never end. Stop waiting for the day when "you can relax" or when "your problems will be over." That day will never come. Most good things in life are fleeting and transitory. Enjoy them; savor them. Don't waste time looking forward to the "happy ending" to all your troubles.

Guideline 12
Don't look back; something might be gaining on you.
—Satchel Paige

Our personal pasts are inhabited largely by ghosts that are of no use to us in our present lives. These ghosts are often circumstances to try to blame for our inadequacies, parental standards to try to live up to, or inaccurate memories of the "good old days." To focus on the past is to rob the present of its joy and vitality.

changing beliefs

Bob was an engineer-turned-executive in his middle thirties. Over the past couple of years he had discovered administrative talents he never suspected he possessed. An experimental fling as a marketing executive for a five-state area proved highly profitable for his company and gave him a bright future, if he wanted it, with this or some other corporation.

Just as his career was starting to take off, Bob privately began to feel increasingly dissatisfied with the way his life was going. He had always worked long hours and been a somewhat driven person. Until recently, the drama of fighting to surmount business challenges was exciting, and more than compensated for the sacrifices and stress involved in the struggle. As a matter of fact, that struggle seemed to be what life was all about. Now he was beginning to tire of the endless contests, and felt he was losing sight of whatever goal or payoff all of his exertion was supposed to be aimed at.

Bob had always been a competitive individual who tended to be impatient with himself and others. He liked to see things done quickly and well. He disliked laziness or inefficiency. He felt a little intolerant of people who, from his point of view, seemed to worry fruitlessly or just mark time in the face of some difficulty. He preferred to solve the problem, or at least get control of the situation, as quickly as possible. Bob was a friendly and generous person whose critical feelings about others had rarely shown until lately. As his own frustration grew, he found it more and more difficult to restrain his impatience with others. He became visibly irritated more and more often with his wife for certain little mistakes, with "pointless, bullshit meetings at work," and with friends and colleagues for "whining" about their problems. Bob had especial difficulty restraining his impatience with his older son, age eleven, who was becoming noticeably fearful and inhibited in the face of his father's frequent criticism, and who perceived Bob's disapproval even when it was not expressed in words.

Weeks and months passed, one very much like another, with no real pleasure in living. Frustration mounted. Uncharacteristically, one morning when caught in traffic on the way to the office, Bob lost his temper, pounded the steering wheel, and cursed out loud at no one in particular. After the outburst, feeling some relief for a moment, he thought to himself, "I used to fight problems; now I seem to be fighting time itself, and I'm losing."

A few days later at a party, Bob fell into a heated discussion with (as he referred to them later) two "intellectual snobs" who criticized certain of his political beliefs. They had him outgunned in terms of facts and, he felt, tried to make a fool out of him in front of the other people present. Bob went home furious. He had not felt so completely helpless for years. What little sleep he got that night was marred by dreams of being publicly ridiculed while helpless to retaliate or protect himself in any way. He woke up several times with intense feelings of panic and shame that passed quickly, but were acutely painful while they lasted.

The next morning, feeling rather drained and lost, Bob did something quite uncustomary for him. He wandered into his four-year-old daughter's room and played on the floor with her, relaxed and idle, for over an hour. After a while some painful thoughts about the previous night's incident came to mind again, bringing tears to his eyes. Despite his efforts to hold them back, his daughter noticed the tears. She did not seem disturbed at all but, to his utter surprise, immediately walked over to him, put her hand on his cheek as if to comfort him, looked into his eyes, and said, "Oh, Daddy, you don't have to cry. I love you." Then he really began to cry, and the two of them were eventually hugging, rolling on the floor, crying, and laughing for a long time.

That evening Bob went for a walk by himself. He reflected on his family, his career, his past. He pictured himself at twenty, an idealistic young man, full of hope and conviction. What had happened to that young man? "What do I want from my life?" Bob blurted aloud, asking no one in particular. He realized that he had no ready answer to his question. He felt lost. It seemed certain to him that something was fundamentally wrong with his basic attitude toward life.

Bob's story is not unusual. Many of us spend years moving from one challenge or responsibility to another without really considering where that motion is taking us. Often we seem to lose our sense of direction, becoming more tense and frustrated. Sometimes, if we are lucky, we may begin to understand that it is our beliefs and values that are creating many of our problems. This recognition is only a beginning step in reducing stress. It is also necessary to learn how to identify and change stress-producing beliefs.

What Are Beliefs?

In this chapter we will outline some effective, easily learned methods for becoming aware of and changing the kinds of mistaken beliefs that generate stress and emotional arousal. It may be helpful to begin with a few words about the nature of beliefs. Mistaken ideas about the nature of beliefs are often problems in their own right. We commonly think that the most important thing about beliefs is whether they are true or false. On the contrary, the most important thing about beliefs is not their truthfulness, but their usefulness. It can be enormously helpful to you to evaluate beliefs in terms of their usefulness rather than their truth or falsehood. Stress-related beliefs are more like value judgments than beliefs about facts. In a real sense, there is no objective way to determine their truthfulness. Beliefs are more or less fruitful guides to action that need to be evaluated based on their results. They are nothing more or less than either effective or ineffective tools for living. The pertinent question is, do your beliefs maximize self-respect and pleasure in living? Little else matters.

Changing one's basic beliefs can be difficult, but such change is a common occurrence. A crucial success or failure experience can dramatically alter one's self-image. Certain of our beliefs and values may shift markedly when we join a new organization or shift professions, so that we are now looking at things from a new perspective. Travel, a new friendship, or falling in love can transform our outlook. Psychotherapy clients often are able to replace life-long self-hatred with self-acceptance as the result of a few months of diligent reconsideration of their self-evaluative beliefs. Most of our beliefs are rather flimsy, with little to support them. They can and should change as new information or needs arise. Even the most deep-seated belief can be altered rapidly when the circumstances are favorable for change.

Please read through this entire chapter before experimenting with any of the specific exercises suggested below. We emphasize several kinds of written records and exercises because they have proven to be invaluable aids to belief change for many persons, especially in the case of do-it-yourself change projects. In later sections we give examples of some simple worksheets and completed sample exercises. You may, however, wish to read only to get a general grasp of belief change principles. We have tried to provide the necessary detail for those who wish to experiment with the written exercises and mental imagery techniques presented below, but not so much detail as to interfere with just reading this chapter for its key ideas.

Identifying Stressful Situations

We encourage you to think of stressful situations very broadly as any life situation that chronically bothers, irritates, or upsets you. We are concerned, not with unusual crises or upheavals, but with the smaller, unavoidable, recurrent stresses of daily life that preoccupy you and keep you tense and on edge. The infallible indicators of stress are (1) worried anticipation of future events that cannot be avoided, and (2) being preoccupied with and ruminating about these events for a period of time after they occur. Anything that you worry about in advance or ruminate about afterward counts as a stressful situation and would be worth analyzing by the methods described in this chapter.

Start out by making a comprehensive list of situations or events you find stressful. Most situations can be described with a single phrase, although some may require several phrases or a couple of sentences. Be very specific—name the exact situation. And be sure to be comprehensive. Do not neglect any area of daily life, however ordinary, or any specific situation you commonly find disturbing.

As you make these situation and theme lists, do not worry about trying to understand why you are bothered or what you can do about it—that comes later. Here are some examples of the tremendously wide range of events that individuals find stressful: driving down the highway; being criticized, unfairly or not, by a supervisor; talking to an attractive member of the opposite sex; having to shave every morning; going to a busy supermarket; writing letters; having a deadline for some work; hearing about someone else's success; talking before a group; disciplining children; having thoughts about being alone; and so forth. Your personal list, of course, can get even more specific in terms of people and places, including items like, "Filling out my weekly time and activities log for the district supervisor," or "Telling George I don't want to go to his close friend Harry's (whom I can't stand) party Saturday night." Make as complete a list as you can. Keep this list and add to it if any additional situations occur to you.

Next, look over your list of specific stress situations and see if you can find a few general themes running through them, or a few general categories in which a number of the stressful events can be placed. You do not need to be overly precise or compulsive about this; just see if some common themes emerge. Some examples might be: situations calling for assertiveness or standing up for your rights; being evaluated by others; close relationships; anything competitive; romantic or sexual situations; performing in public; confusing or busy situations; deadlines; etc. Write down the common themes as they occur to you. They will give you a helpful overview of your experience of stress.

Detecting Perceptions of Threat

The next step is to select a representative stressful situation for you, or one that is currently bothering you, and try to make some kind of new sense out of it. Step back from your experience of this situation for a moment and reconsider what is really happening. Stop experiencing everything so immediately and urgently. You probably are making a lot of assumptions that are faulty and need to be reconsidered. Your perceptions of threat or infringement in this situation, not the situation itself, are the source of stress. It would be helpful for you to ask yourself these questions: What exactly do I experience as stressful in this situation? Can I put into words precisely what I find to be frightening or irritating in it? What specifically am I telling myself about this stressful incident that makes it have the meaning it does for me and causes me to feel the way I do about it? Can I really see the situation as one that I make disturbing by the meaning I give it, rather than as an episode that automatically or directly makes me feel distressed?

The best way to get in touch with the threatening or hostile meanings you give to events is to become aware of what you say to yourself about them. The things you tell yourself about what is happening, what it means, what is going to happen next, and what you should do about it create and maintain perceptions of infringement and threat. Your self-talk and self-instructions stoke the emotional furnace and keep the coals glowing.

In the stressful situation you have selected, try to become aware of the way you interpret the people and events involved. Determine what is the most stressful moment for you in this situation, for example, "Facing a deadline at work." Often the most stressful point is anticipating a situation while sitting around waiting for it to occur. Sometimes the most disturbing moment is thinking about an event after it occurs. Focus on yourself at that moment and become aware of the kinds of thoughts and images that cross your mind. You have probably been through it all many times. Imagine that there is a videotape with soundtrack of your images and self-talk at that point in time. Replay it several times in your imagination.

Write down on the left half of a worksheet, like the one on

page 97, as many as you can of the things you say or picture to yourself in that situation. Be specific and comprehensive. Do not take anything for granted. Many of the things you tell yourself that cause anxiety or irritation have become so automatic and familiar that it will be difficult to disconnect the public facts from the meaning you give to them. Be especially alert for self-talk containing the words *should, must, ought to, deserve, owe,* or any of their negatives or synonyms. These kinds of rights and obligations are not part of the objective situation. They are meanings you give to it. If you feel that something is missing from your picture or the situation, crystallized in your internal monologue of self-talk, then it probably is. Look again. Generate as much self-talk as you can, even minor variations on themes, until you have a comprehensive list. (Ignore the right half of this worksheet until later.)

The thoughts and images you have written down reveal the perceptions of threat that trigger the stress reaction. They also provide clues, which, if read properly, can eventually lead you to the mistaken beliefs that are the source of much stress.

Worksheet 1

SITUATION   Facing an office deadline

Negative Self-Talk	Positive Self-Talk
"I'll never get finished."	"Just take it one step at a time."
"If I miss this I've really blown it."	"Some tension is inevitable but I don't have to worry about it."
"Why am I so anxious, I hate feeling like this."	"I really do have confidence in my basic ability. What else matters?"
(Picturing missing the deadline and things falling apart.)	"Mistakes happen. Let the future take care of itself."
(Thinking about someone else who could probably do a better job.)	"Don't anticipate problems, just get started."
"I *must* get going, I *must* hurry."	"What's reasonable for today —just do it!"
"What will people think if I fall behind? No one will say anything, but I just know what they will think!"	"You did a good piece of work today—take pleasure in it."
"What's the best way to proceed? A mistake may cost me too much time to get finished."	"You handled the stress well. Be proud of it!"
"I hate myself."	
Etc.	

Identifying Goal Conflicts

Often the events that disturb us most are those that indicate to us that we will either not reach goals, or will reach them with great difficulty. You may experience stress because you have set for yourself a goal that is unrealistic and cannot be reached (like being nearly perfect), or because you have embraced two or more goals that are incompatible (like effectively disciplining your children but having them never get mad at you). Often what appears to be simply a single, unrealistic goal in living turns out, on closer examination, to be a goal conflict. Perfectionists commonly want both to be nearly perfect in everything they do *and* be relaxed, tolerant persons who really enjoy being alive.

Select an area of stress in which you have tried to detect perceptions of threat by becoming aware of your arousing self-talk. You can usually deduce what some of your most important goals must be (or confirm what you already know about them) by figuring out what aim or ambition is hindered by the event that disturbs you. Generally speaking, our perceptions of threat are more reliable guides to what is important to us than our lists of New Year's resolutions or other statements for public consumption. For example, if you find it quite disturbing that several acquaintances seem to have taken a dislike to you, then you probably want to be popular with nearly everyone—admit it or not.

Stress-related goals may be a source of chronic frustration for you because reaching them demands that you exercise more control over present circumstances or future outcomes than is humanly possible. Being nearly perfect, being liked by nearly everyone, never making a big mistake or a fool out of yourself, guaranteeing your own future success or your children's happiness, being on top of every social situation, and feeling secure almost all of the time are examples of such goals. Often such goals are excessively future-oriented. By adopting them you put yourself under stress both by straining to reach an impossible future and by giving up so much of the pleasure available in the present.

Stress may also be the inevitable byproduct of adopting goals that conflict with one another. We often give roughly equal allegiance to two major goals in living that are incompatible with one another, clash, and make us highly vulnerable to stress. We pay a price for trying to have our cake and eat it too. Conflicting goals may simply demand more time and energy than is available, as when one tries to be a full-time parent to two or three children while pursing an interesting and demanding career. Or, our goals may involve incompatible values, such as getting ahead professionally or financially as quickly as possible, while being basically honest with everyone and never taking advantage of them. Can you paint a mental picture of how different segments of your life (thoughts, feelings, and actions) are organized around efforts to reach goals that cannot be reached or that clash with one another, thus producing stress? Write down some of your thoughts about the goal conflicts you uncover.

Finding Mistaken Beliefs

You have become aware of some of your perceptions of threat and noted how they may be related to certain unrealistic or conflicting goals. Now you are in a position to press to a deeper level of understanding by trying to find the mistaken belief or beliefs that are the ultimate source of these stress-producing goals and disturbing perceptions of everyday events. Look over the notes you have made to yourself concerning your self-talk and goal strivings. Using the mistaken beliefs we have discussed in earlier chapters as a starting point, try to discern what kinds of faulty beliefs are expressed by your self-talk and the meanings you give to disturbing events. Take any unrealistic goal in living you have clarified and try to explain to yourself why you pursue this goal. Do this by finding the mistaken assumption about self-esteem, emotional security, etc., that makes it necessary for you to value this goal highly, even supremely, in your day-to-day life. Try to find a mistaken belief that makes sense out of your tendency to worry a great deal, live in the future, evaluate yourself or your performances harshly, experience excessive anger and frustration, or whatever form stressful living is taking for you.

On a second worksheet like the one on page 101, write down in personally convincing language a statement of the underlying mistaken belief that seems to be involved in the experience of stress you are examining. Try to come up with a succinct, meaningful statement of the belief that seems to underlie your perceptions of infringement or threat in that situation. (Suggestions for using the remainder of the worksheet are found later in this chapter.)

Some further remarks about the nature of faulty, stress-related beliefs may help you identify and articulate them. Mistaken beliefs that cause emotional turmoil are all, in a sense, false. But they are not false in the way that the statement, "The pages of this book are green," or the belief, "Water boils at 300 degrees Fahrenheit," are false. It is not possible simply to compare such beliefs or their predictions with the facts so that an objective observer could see they are incorrect. They are more subtle and insidious than that.

There are two basic kinds of faulty, stress-related beliefs. Which category a belief belongs to depends largely on whether it is stated in the third or the first person. Examples of beliefs stated in the third person are, "Some people are more worthwhile than others," "Success is happiness," "It is always devastating to lose a lover or spouse," and so forth. Such beliefs are not so much false as nonsensical. They are unverifiable. Notwithstanding the fact that many of us try to live by them, they cannot be proven or disproven. For example, someone says he feels inferior to you and to most people and that this is the reason he is unhappy. You reply by reminding him about a mutual acquaintance who seems quite ordinary but lives very happily. He responds by saying something like, "Ah, but he is not really inferior. He has a wife who loves him, which is more than I have." There are a sufficient number of ordinary, unsuccessful, happy people and extraordinary, successful unhappy people to keep the argument going forever.

Mistaken beliefs stated in the first person are the most detrimental ones. Some examples are, "I am a loser," "No one could ever love me," and "I have to fight for everything I get in this dog-eat-dog world." Such beliefs are also unverifiable: There is no way to prove or disprove them. But they have an important additional quality. They are self-fulfilling prophe-

Worksheet 2

SITUATION <u>Feeling shy and "out of it" in social situations</u>

1. Mistaken Belief (in your own personal words).

Most people aren't interested in knowing me or having me in their circle of friends. I lack something important.

2. Alternative Calm and Realistic Belief (personally convincing words).

I have the potential to be most of the things I would ever really want to be. Nothing stands between me and other people unless I hold myself back. I am what I am, and I can find no good reason not to like it.

3. Notes on how you would specifically think, behave, and feel differently if you replaced (1) with (2).

More comfortable and outgoing in social situations and with friends. Less fantasy and more doing. Less critical of others' little faults. Stop reading in personal references to myself. Stop calling myself names like "stupid" and "dull." Trust my own instincts in conversation, just say what I think in a relaxed way and follow it out. Stop making such a big deal out of it when I say something "dumb." Socialize more to give more chances for fun, but don't expect anything great out of a particular occasion. Treat people as equals—don't magnify or belittle them. Return phone calls more promptly, just get them out of the way. Take that occasional whine out of my voice, etc.

cies. They exert a profound influence on the course of events. They cause you to perceive selectively only those facts that seem to support your negative or stressful view. And they lead you to behave in ways that arrange your world to conform to your stress-producing belief. If you angrily press and fight for most of the things you want, you may create a tense, dog-eat-dog social environment. The truth of these beliefs is often arbitrary and self-created.

The main purpose of beliefs, of course, is not to be true. We are mainly not detached knowers but involved actors who are trying to accomplish something with our beliefs. Stress-producing beliefs keep us aroused and fighting against obstacles or alert and on guard against possible threat. That is their purpose. The question is, do they bring us anything of value? And, is it worth the price?

Self-Persuasion

Changing one's beliefs is, at its core, a process of self-persuasion. We must persuade ourselves to face certain realities that are not always what we would like them to be, and then persuade ourselves to try some new, more effective approach to dealing with them.

Creating New Beliefs. Return to the worksheet on page 101 and endeavor to criticize and reconsider the mistaken belief you have identified. Briefly look over your notes once again concerning self-talk and goal· strivings related to situations where this belief comes into play. Try to look at the incidents that characteristically disturb you. See if you can reinterpret them in a way that makes them seem less disturbing or irritating.

When you feel ready to do so, write out a brief statement of an alternative, calming, more realistic belief that might guide your responding in a threatfree way to the situations you are analyzing. It is very important that this belief seem plausible to you and be stated in your own words and in personally convincing language. You must be able to sense the desirability of seeing the world in these less disturbing terms, even though you may not yet be able to keep to that view at all times under stress.

A new outlook opens up the possiblity of new modes of

coping with new, more satisfying results. Flesh out your picture of the world from this new perspective by making some written notes to yourself specifically concerning how you would think, behave, and feel differently if you replaced your mistaken belief with a more calming one. Think of concrete new actions that would typically follow this positive shift in your perception of the stressful situation.

Changing Self-Talk. Persuading yourself to think and act differently will involve talking differently to yourself as you confront potentially stressful events. Go back to the first worksheet and generate examples of what would be, for you, positive calming task-oriented self-talk in the situations you are scrutinizing. It is important to cultivate and emphasize the positive. Most people tend to be general and negative, rather than specific and positive, when they address the task of fashioning a new outlook. They try to reduce stress by saying to themselves things like, "I shouldn't be so anxious when I arrive at work in the morning." A more effective message would be, "It is highly unlikely that I would make a serious mistake in this situation, and if I did, even that would not be difficult to correct—let me start the day with a piece of work that needs to be done and just get involved in it." The next time you are in that stressful situation, try using the self-talk you have generated. Actively attempt to calm yourself down by making statements to yourself that help you reinterpret the situation in a positive manner.

Sometimes it is difficult to become aware of arousal-producing self-talk or develop calming alternative self-statements because we often take a threatened view of events in an almost instantaneous, automatic manner. In these cases, no specific internal statement can be readily identified. However, in the case of a threatened outlook, you can usually step back from your perception of the situation, notice what it is like, and say something like, "I am viewing this situation as if I were saying to myself, 'This is dangerous,' or 'I may fail at that.'" Something very much like that sort of self-statement is occurring, even if almost instantaneously. Putting this implicit self-talk into words as best you can will work very well for the purposes of these exercises and for changing your beliefs.

Ongoing Self-Disputation. Active, energetic, repeated self-disputation is an exceedingly important part of successful self-persuasion. It is necessary to dispute your faulty, stress-producing assumption and beliefs regularly. We are exposed daily to so many bad examples and so much misinformation about managing emotions, finding happiness, and the sources of self-esteem that it takes a concerted effort to think straight. If you are currently making some changes in coping with stress, we strongly suggest that you set aside fifteen minutes a day to sit quietly by yourself, reflect on these changes, and actively dispute the erroneous thinking that will tend to leak back in and undermine your change efforts. You might wish to practice progressive relaxation or meditation (See Chapters 10 and 11) for fifteen or twenty minutes, followed by fifteen minutes of unstructured self-disputation in which you calmly try to get in touch with faulty beliefs and actively criticize them. It is important to be alone with yourself during the argument. You can tell you are getting somewhere if occasionally your mood shifts noticeably and you feel more securely anchored within yourself. An especially good program for many persons is to relax or meditate every day, followed by either a self-disputation session or, on alternate days, by application of one of the mental imagery methods described later in this chapter.

There is no precise formula for effective self-disputation. But it always involves asking yourself, and trying to answer, the kinds of questions that help you detect perceptions of threat and faulty assumptions. What specific incidents preoccupy and distress me? What am I worrying about that keeps me under some degree of tension? Can I interrupt the flow of my experiences and pause to reconsider for a moment? Do I have to perceive things that way? Can I be calm for a moment, reconsider, and get anxious or angry again only if it really seems appropriate? Can I see how stress is the inevitable consequence of the way I view these situations? Therefore, can I stop worrying about stress, or perhaps even blaming myself for feeling it, and turn my attention to changing my attitude and perceptions? Can I see how some of my attempts to cope with stress have been ineffective because they did not get to its source in a really basic goal or belief? Have I been willing to question every belief or commitment except for one or two I have avoided looking at closely? Can I look at those sensitive matters now? If a belief is inconsistent with my health or happiness, can I consider discarding it? Can I stop making any excuse that attributes the cause of my discomfort to outside factors I cannot cope with more effectively? If the thought of eliminating excuses makes me despair of things ever being different, can I remind myself that such despair probably comes from having viewed myself in the past as a victim of stressful events or my own emotional reactions to them? Is it difficult for me to reevaluate my attitude because I sense that if I change my attitude or approach I may have to take some new action, or give something up, that frightens me? Might that fear not also dissolve if it were examined calmly and rationally? Is it worth the risk to examine and see?

Taking New Action

Taking new action is critical for attitude or belief change. Challenging old beliefs can stir up a great deal of hope. But new, more calming beliefs are fragile and tenuous. One moment they fill you with confidence and pleasant anticipation. The next moment they seem implausible or even ridiculous as a sense of fear or anger returns and colors your outlook once again. New beliefs require evidence to support them. They require hard facts and undeniable experiences to confirm their validity and usefulness. This kind of evidence is available. But it comes only in the form of the feedback that results from taking new action. The results of behaving in new ways in old, familiar, threatening situations can be the discovery that feared consequences do not happen, or that they do and it is possible to cope with them in a worryfree manner.

Everyone knows how terribly important a positive self-image and sense of self-confidence are in every sector of life. If you see yourself as likable and competent you will experience little anxiety and find yourself behaving in a relaxed and dauntless manner that is very attractive to most other people and creates more opportunities for interesting things to do than you have the time to take advantage of. If you are self-doubting and hesitant, however, such opportunities seem scarce and you are able to pursue them only at the price of a certain amount of stress. How can one build self-confidence? How can one create the positive self-image that leads one to expect favorable outcomes and even helps bring them to pass?

One way to build self-confidence is to rid your thinking of the mistaken beliefs and inveterate self-evaluation that cause you to perceive certain happenings or the actions of others as a threat to your well-being. Then there are no reasons for taking a constricted view of life's possibilities, and no barrier to bold, spontaneous action. Then nothing stands between you and creative absorption in things you really care about. There is another side, however, to the problem of building a positive self-image. According to an old saying, it is easier to act your way into a new way of thinking than to think your way into a new way of acting. A very unfortunate myth has it that you must build up a critical mass of self-confidence before you can take the risk of behaving differently in key life situations. If that were true, few efforts at change would get past the stage of wishful thinking. The fact that new actions may be uncertain, awkward, and ineffective is not a problem unless you believe that you need everything to go smoothly and efficiently the first time through. If you can accept clumsiness and moments of great uncertainty as a natural part of living that in no way disparages you as a person, then you may begin to see ways to build a solid sense of self-esteem gradually through new action of many different kinds.

Some very interesting psychological research suggests that we form much of our self-picture in the same way that we form impressions and judgments about other people. We perceive ourselves reacting in the ways we do. Then we make inferences concerning what kind of persons with what kind of capabilities we must be, given the fact that we behave this way. These conclusions concerning what we are like or capable of, of course, can profoundly influence our future behavior. Thus, someone who behaves in a weak and unassertive manner may observe his own actions and their effects and draw the conclusion that he is a rather unimpressive individual who is vulnerable to having his rights trampled on by other people. This may lead him to shun conflict and withdraw from people in general for fear of being hurt.

The idea that we fashion our self-image according to our perceptions of how we actually behave in important life situations takes a lot of the mystery out of the notion of self-image and its influence upon us. It also opens up some exciting avenues for change. The unassertive individual just described might not draw the inference that he is an inherently weak person who cannot protect himself or get what he wants out of life. He might decide (correctly) that his problems are due to weak behavior, not to some mystical weak "personality," and that by changing his behavior he can not only prevent being walked on, but start building a very gratifying image of himself as a strong and self-assured person.

A poor self-image or lack of self-confidence is usually an accurate reflection of a disorganized or ineffective style of living. It is unreasonable to expect a change in our picture of ourselves until there is a change in the way of living upon which it is based. This is true even for a perfectionist who evaluates herself harshly because she is not nearly perfect in everything she does. A positive self-image does not come from superior accomplishments or being better than other people. It comes from living in a relaxed, charitable, outgoing manner, with an awareness of one's limitations and a sense of humor about one's own and others' failings. Perfectionists rarely have a well-managed life style. Straining after perfection tends to prevent spontaneity, adaptability, inner calm, and a balanced way of life—yet these are the very qualities that make up a positive self-image.

A glimpse of the world from a new perspective needs to be followed immediately by new behavior, hopefully by a sustained effort to forge a style of living that will keep you relatively free of stress. No amount of positive thinking, positive talking, or getting prepared to make a change sometime in the indefinite future will substitute for the action that usually is possible today. A shift in attitude always means that you will behave differently in some specific, stressful situation that you encounter in everyday life. Often there is one key action that seems to symbolize a new approach. It may be asserting yourself with some individual, simply ignoring someone's remarks, taking a whole day off to do nothing but enjoy yourself, not putting something off until the last minute, refusing to worry yourself into a headache over some matter—the possibilities are endless. But they all have in common the fact that, for you personally, in these particular circumstances, they symbolize (1) taking charge of the situation by dealing directly with a problem or doing what you really want to do, and (2) refusing to worry about or be emotionally disturbed by things you cannot anticipate or control. If such a key action occurs to you, do it! It will cement your new perspective and may lead to further insights.

The next step is to move ahead as quickly as possible in fashioning an overall style of living that keeps stress at a minimum. Doing that in today's world requires a great deal of persistence and personal creativity. Everyone, though, is capable of carrying through on such a project. You may find some of the principles set forth in earlier chapters concerning managing one's life style and resolving interpersonal conflict helpful in developing a relatively stressfree way of living.

The remainder of this section and the following section on imagery methods describe specific methods of overcoming inertia and blocks to taking the kind of new action indicated by new beliefs. Many people find these kinds of structured techniques especially helpful during periods of major change in their outlook or approach to coping with stress. These techniques give you something to do when you are stuck. Sometimes you can decide to try one of these techniques when you know you need a fresh perspective but cannot seem to acquire it, or when you are having difficulty taking some kind of new action immediately that you think would pay off in the long run.

Making use of a diary can help you promote awareness and change of stressful beliefs. Keeping a diary of your reactions to stress for a period of time can compensate for the fact that we are generally poor observers of our own behavior. We often forget unpleasant moments or undesirable behaviors soon after they occur. We naturally tend to distort our recollection of many events so that it will accord more closely with our beliefs or what we wanted to happen. As a result, it is difficult to make the kind of realistic evaluation of a potentially stressful situation that is needed if we are going to revise our appraisal of it.

Keeping a Diary. Try keeping a simple diary of stressful events and your reactions to them in an ordinary ring or spiral-type notebook. Use a page per day with a simple format like the following. Down the lefthand side of the page, write down, each day, a phrase or sentence describing any incidents or situations you find stressful. Opposite these incidents, down the righthand side of the page, make notes to yourself concerning your thoughts, feelings, and behavior in these situations. Record any other comments that occur to you.

After keeping the diary for about a week, set aside a little time to look over your notes. See if you can notice any interesting patterns that emerge over a day or a period of days. You may notice situations you were not previously aware bothered you, or features of your self-talk or behavior that escaped your attention until now. You may wish to subject new situations to closer examination, or reexamine familiar ones afresh, in the light of this new information. A diary and periodic review of this sort provide you with much information that is difficult to obtain any other way. It allows you to extend the written methods for disputing and restructuring beliefs described in this chapter over a longer span of time, and can be a powerful tool for self-change.

Self-Monitoring. Techniques of self-monitoring can also provide you with useful information and help you change persistent negative habits. Psychological research has found that keeping a careful, systematic record of one's behavior in specific situations can facilitate changing one's response to that situation. Self-monitoring typically involves carrying with you a small notebook, or several 3 × 5 index cards, and recording the number of times, the time of day, and the circumstances under which a certain behavior (either desired or undesired) occurs. Just make three columns per page or card. Put times of the day down the leftmost column, use the middle column for making a mark each time the behavior occurs, and use the rightmost column for notes concerning circumstances, your reactions to them, and other comments.

This method has been used to keep a record of such varied behaviors as cigarettes smoked or urges to smoke, angry remarks, depressed thoughts, times you wanted to assert yourself and did not, compulsive scratching, striking up a conversation, and many others.

Some examples of behaviors commonly associated with stress that might be monitored are: acting assertively or unassertively in interpersonal situations, thoughts or fantasies comparing your achievements or qualities with those of others, avoiding potential conflict situations that need to be dealt with, fearful rumination about losing a relationship, worrying about what others think about you, thoughtlessly adding activities or appointments to your schedule, doing something relaxing or simply fun, procrastinating or not procrastinating, saying "No" to unreasonable requests made of you, initiating conversation or social interactions, and unnecessary critical thoughts or remarks about other people. Many of the specific actions that you note changing a stress-producing belief would also make appropriate targets for self-monitoring.

Here are some guidelines for selecting and monitoring stress-related behaviors. Select behaviors, even if they are thoughts or fantasies, that are sufficiently specific and discrete that you can count their frequency and keep a roughly accurate tally of the number of times they occur on a daily basis. Self-monitor a selected behavior for at least a week. Your record may provide new information about the circumstances that provoke a stressful response or put you in touch with features of your behavior or self-talk that you were unaware of before. Review the record daily in order to glean this kind of information from it. If there is not a noticeable decrease or increase (whichever is appropriate) in the target behavior within a period of two to three weeks, you should consider the possibility that your grasp of the underlying attitude leading to stress in this situation is incomplete. Or, it may be that some other aspect of your behavior needs to alter before the one you are monitoring can be brought into line. As the frequency of some persistent negative habit or reaction goes down, you might switch to monitoring a positive response to the same potentially stressful situation. The feedback you receive by doing this can be rewarding and stimulate creativity. Thus, you might switch from monitoring angry reactions to criticism to recording calm, nondefensive responses to these same remarks of others and writing down comments about the positive results you obtain from this new style of interaction.

Fixed Role Technique. Finally, you may wish to experiment with a fixed role technique for changing your approach to coping with stress. Fixed role techniques have proven useful for many psychotherapy clients. Also, many people seem to arrive on their own at similar means, without using that name, of course, for changing entrenched patterns of behavior.

Select a pattern of behavior that you feel contributes to stress in your life. For a period of time, preferably at least a week, reverse that pattern and behave in an entirely different or opposite manner in every part of your life where the pattern appears. For example, suppose you have a tendency to procrastinate both in many little matters and when faced with major tasks and deadlines. (Such a pattern, by the way, is a common symptom of stress. We try to escape pressure and drivenness by putting things off for a while, but never really enjoy the momentary escape from the inevitable—it is no substitute for genuine playfulness, fun, or intrinsically meaningful activities.) For a week or two play the part, morning and night, of someone who never puts things off, uses small amounts of available time to get something done without ever rationalizing that it is not enough, works hard for a reasonable period of time and then forgets work to play hard or relax, does what can be done without worrying at all about what cannot be accomplished at the moment, and so forth. Throw yourself into the role. Do not think in terms of gradual or partial changes to test things out, but commit yourself to acting that part with enthusiasm and rigor for the designated time. (You can always revert to your old ways when the experiment is finished.) Above all, do not ruminate about slipups, relapses, or feelings of awkwardness as you carry out the role. Return immediately to your role in the manner of a self-confident actor who merely flubbed a line and would never allow it to hold up the play.

Sometimes it is easier to throw yourself wholly into such a role than measure out change in small doses, having to rethink the issues with each new step. Enacting the role in a fixed or unrelenting manner for an extended period of time also gives you the richest possible experience of a potentially more rewarding approach. This experience can effectively disconfirm mistaken beliefs that suggest such a new approach might lead to difficulty or disaster.

Imagery Techniques

There is a growing awareness in many branches of psychology of the importance of mental imagery. Our mental pictures and fantasies exert an enormous influence upon our lives. Our perceptions of infringement or threat often are crystallized in images of stressful events. Our mistaken beliefs about ourselves and the outcomes of events often take the form of fantasies about what will happen and how we and others will be affected if we behave in certain ways.

In changing reactions to stress it is often helpful to make a deliberate effort to alter some of the imagery associated with perceptions of threat. Generally speaking, this involves (1) becoming aware of stress-related imagery; (2) developing new, more adaptive patterns of imagery and fantasy; and (3) practice in using the new imagery to guide threatfree responses to potentially stressful events. In this section we will describe two procedures for restructuring stress-related imagery, namely coping imagery and prolonged imaginal exposure. Most individuals can apply these techniques on their own by following the guidelines presented and drawing on skills, such as progressive relaxation, that are described elsewhere in this book.

Each of the following imagery methods involves imaginally confronting a stressful situation a number of times over without either giving way to panic or retreating from the scene. This may not be possible in a situation involving severe fear reactions. In these cases it can be preferable to approach the situation very gradually, starting with scenes that are quite remote in space or time from the actual frightening situation. The assistance of a professional therapist is desirable in carrying this out, and may be necessary if you are to arrive at a correct and thorough analysis of the fear problem. However, you should have no difficulty in experimenting with these imagery methods when overwhelming negative emotions are not involved.

Coping Imagery. First, select one of the stressful situations you are currently trying to master. Select one you have already analyzed in terms of arousal-producing self-talk and mistaken beliefs in the manner described earlier in this chapter. This basic exercise takes about fifteen minutes to complete. You may wish to extend it to as much as forty-five minutes in order to repeat a particular scene a number of additional times, or cover several different situations in one exercise session.

Secondly, find a place where you can lie down, be very comfortable, and not be disturbed. Take five to ten minutes to become very relaxed and calm. You may wish to use the progressive relaxation or meditation techniques described later to reach a tranquil state. Become very relaxed while remaining mentally alert, and let yourself enjoy the relaxation thoroughly.

Third, after you have achieved a relaxed state of body and mind, with your eyes closed visualize the stressful situation you have selected in the following manner. Picture yourself approaching or in the situation. At first you begin to get a little anxious or angrily disturbed, you start to worry or fret, and you feel the very beginnings of whatever physical symptoms of arousal you commonly feel in this kind of situation. But right away you interrupt the process of getting anxious or disturbed and take measures to counteract it. You relax physically in the scene, perhaps taking in a deep breath and slowly letting it out. And you tell yourself to relax and not to worry, but just to deal calmly with the situation, one step at a time. Finally, in the scene you relax, turn your attention away from worries, cope smoothly with the situation, get yourself really to feel undisturbed and confident, and perhaps move on to doing something else.

In other words, if it is an anxious scene, you allow yourself to become just a little bit anxious (or to experience only the initial stages of anxiety), and then you counteract anxiety with (1) physical and emotional relaxation, and (2) calming self-instructions and self-talk. To summarize, the steps in using coping imagery are:

1. Select an appropriate stressful situation.
2. Get comfortable and relaxed.
3. Visualize yourself coping effectively. In the scene
   a. begin to get disturbed and/or worry.
   b. relax physically and emotionally.
   c. tell yourself to relax, not to worry, and to be-
      have in a calm and deliberate manner.
   d. cope effectively with the situation.
   e. really get yourself to feel calm and confident.

It usually takes about thirty to sixty seconds to complete a single scene. Visualize the sequence from your beginning to get anxious through your coping effectively. Then stop visualizing the scene, and turn your attention briefly back to relaxation. Forget about the scene entirely and take about one minute to relax completely once again. Do not go on until you are pretty completely relaxed once more. Then repeat the scene. If all goes well, visualize the same scene at least four or five times from beginning to end. You may wish to visualize the scene an additional five to ten times, however. Or, you may wish to go ahead and visualize one or two additional scenes in the same manner. Concentrate on just a few scenes and visualize them a number of times, until you are very comfortable with them, before moving on to other scenes. The mark of successful visualization of a scene is that you actually change your feelings and thoroughly become calm and self-possessed.

When you visualize yourself coping effectively with this potentially stressful event, try to imagine yourself really in the situation. That is, so far as possible, do not watch yourself from the outside in the scene, but picture it as if you were really there, seeing the events as they unfold through your own eyes. Picture the scene as clearly and vividly as possible. Also, do not rely only on your sense of sight. Deliberately imagine the scene in terms of all the other senses. Allow yourself to hear sounds, experience odors and tastes associated with the scene, and even let yourself experience some of the physical or kinesthetic sensations that are part of being in that situation.

Some individuals find it helpful to make written notes on their scenes before beginning the exercise. It is also possible to write out a complete set of instructions for visualizing a scene and record them on an audiotape cassette for playback during a coping imagery session. An entire session, including relaxation instructions and scene descriptions, may be recorded for repeated use. Instructions for a typical scene might read as follows:

Imagine yourself about to walk to the front of the room and make a short speech on a policy matter before the XYZ civic organization. Just before it is time to go forward you get a lump in your throat and begin to feel anxious and lightheaded. But you immediately take in a deep breath and let it out slowly. You relax your muscles and feel the chair solidly underneath you. As you walk up tell yourself to just relax and speak naturally without trying to judge your performance every second. You remind yourself that this is just a group of normal human beings like yourself who have no wish to be critical of you. You start to speak, get a feel for the situation, relax and get involved in making the talk, and do a very adequate job of making your points. You become really calm. Now imagine this scene all the way through from the beginning . . . (forty-five seconds) . . . Now stop visualizing the scene and just go back to relaxing once again.

Prolonged Imaginal Exposure. This method is similar to the use of coping imagery, but involves extended or prolonged visualization of a single scene. You may use it for variety or as a matter of preference. We recommend that you try prolonged exposure if you (1) have difficulty visualizing yourself coping effectively with a situation using the coping imagery method, or (2) continue to find the real-life situation stressful despite successful imaginal practice in coping with it.

Most of the guidelines for coping imagery apply to the prolonged exposure method. Select a scene to visualize. Get comfortable. Take five or ten minutes to become very relaxed, and enjoy it. Then picture yourself in the stressful situation as clearly and vividly as possible. Use all your senses and the full powers of your imagination so that it seems as if you really are there.

Continue to imagine yourself in that situation for a full eight to ten minutes. Depending on what kind of situation it is, just remain in it as calmly as possible (for example, listening to someone you don't particularly like talk about his or her success) or cope with it as effectively as you are able (for example, making a speech before a small group of people). Every thirty seconds or so in the scene, relax physically and tell yourself in some appropriate manner not to worry and to take a threatfree view of the situation. Do not exert yourself in trying to cope effectively with the situation or worry about your success at doing so. The emphasis here is simply on remaining in the situation without excessive arousal for a long period of time.

After about ten minutes, stop visualizing the scene and let yourself relax for a minute. Then repeat the exercise once more, imagining the scene for another eight to ten minutes. Limit a session to those two ten-minute exposures to the scene, repeating sessions every day or every few days, as you wish, of relaxation in between. If the situation you are working on is one you find difficult to imagine coping with smoothly, then continue sessions at least until you can visualize yourself fairly calm and handling the situation satisfactorily for a period of two or three minutes. Then you may wish to conclude with a session of briefer visualizations of the scene following the coping imagery method.

It is difficult to expose yourself imaginally for a prolonged period of time to a stressful situation in this manner without dramatically altering your perceptions of the situation. This kind of exposure affords abundant opportunity for rational reevaluation of the threatening character of these events. A number of different insights or shifts in perspective may occur as you imagine scenes using either of these imagery techniques. If you are keeping a stress diary, you may find it interesting and helpful to keep notes on your experiences with these methods.

A Final Word

We must leave it to your individual taste and creativity to select among the many approaches to belief change described in this chapter. Do what interests you. Experiment until you find some techniques that work. Changing one's basic beliefs and the ways of living based on them is a subtle process. These structured techniques and written exercises, however, can help you gain insight into faulty beliefs, revamp them, and translate new attitudes into more effective approaches to coping with stress.

If you are making a concerted effort to reduce stress in your life at this time, an effective program that does not make unreasonable demands upon your time might include the following:

1. Keep a simple stress diary for about a month.
2. Spend four to five hours' time over that month doing some of the written exercises that may assist you in detecting perceptions of threat and faulty beliefs.
3. Set aside a half-hour to forty-five minutes every day or every other day for (a) fifteen to twenty minutes of relaxation or meditation followed by (b) private self-disputation and reflection about stress-related beliefs and patterns of living or application of an imagery technique. (We recommend you continue at least the relaxation or meditation practice for several months.)
4. Experiment once or twice with self-monitoring or fixed role methods, especially if you are having difficulty breaking stress-producing habits or changing entrenched behavior patterns.

managing your life style

In our definition of stress we stated that it is not events in themselves that cause stress but rather our perceptions and evaluations of events. Much of this book has concerned itself with helping you change your reactions to whatever circumstances you find yourself in. It is sometimes feasible, however, to reduce stress by altering the events that lead to the perceptions of stress. This chapter will devote itself to detailing a few simple steps that you can take to make your environment less stressful.

Our behavior—what we do—as much as what we think can either add to or reduce the stress in our lives. If our actions are thoughtfully directed we can create for ourselves a life style that is free from the hurry, worry, and chaos that characterize stressful existences. To carve out a low-stress life style, one must learn how to battle the factors that are at the root of tension and anxiety.

Much stress results from a simple failure to organize our lives effectively. A common complaint among overstressed individuals is that "It just isn't possible for me to do all that I have to do." This belief that there is a shortage of time makes us hurry and worry. Outside pressures seem to impinge upon us, demanding all of our energies and time just to accomplish the things we must do. Failing to find time to do the things we want to, we are frustrated and demoralized. The delayed vacation, the postponed night on the town, the putoff day with the kids are the victims of our poorly organized lives. Our lives often seem to be a series of unending crises and inflexible demands. Many of these demands seem unrelated and unpredictable. The stress mounts.

When we recall our model of stress, it is easy to see that a disorganized, inefficient person would be vulnerable to stress. Stress results from the anticipation of future unpleasantness, especially unpleasantness that we feel we may not be able to cope with. The person who moves from one current demand to another without systematically assessing and planning for future outcomes will inevitably be less certain about how she will handle future demands. Disorganized people often live with a constant sense of impending disaster. At some level they feel that something is about to go wrong (because things have in the past), but they do not know what, how, or when. Stress feeds on this kind of perpetual uncertainty. Inefficient people are often running hard to catch up. They never really feel on top of the tasks their lives seem to require of them. Often they are people in a hurry, people with that sense of time-urgency that has been found to be a key part of the coronary-prone Type A behavior pattern.

In the next few pages we will provide you with some helpful hints for beginning the transition from chaos to order, from inefficiency to efficiency. Even if you consider yourself to be a relatively well-organized person, read on. You might be in for some surprises. For those of you interested in a more thorough treatment of this subject, we highly recommend *How to Get Control of Your Time and Your Life*, by Alan Lakein. His work has served as the inspiration for much of this chapter.

A. *Learn to Plan:* Without planning it is impossible to predict, prepare for, and cope with the future. Planning is the act of deciding what you want to do and how you will go about doing it. All organizations, whether they be industrial, governmental, military, or educational, invest large sums of money in planning what they will do in the future. They spend so much time and effort in planning because they know from experience that without planning, chaos and inefficiency result.

We feel that it is just as important for individuals to plan as it is for large organizations. The future arrives whether we are ready for it or not. Being able to anticipate and meet the demands of the future means one is less vulnerable to stress. The method of planning that we will present here consists of three steps:

1. Selection of Goals
2. Deriving Objectives from Goals
3. Selecting Activities for the Achievement of Objectives

The selection of goals begins with your asking yourself the question, "What do I want out of life?" Start answering this question in terms of broad, general categories. Think about all the things you would like to achieve, obtain, or experience, and then list them. Include anything you feel you want even if it is not realistic or sensible. A list from one of our clients had these items (not in order of priority):

1. Money-wealth
2. Love
3. A good marriage
4. A trip around the world
5. A Mercedes-Benz
6. An affair with Sophia Loren
7. A family
8. Beating Jimmy Connors in tennis
9. To find peace within myself
10. To be well liked

Once you have generated the list, go back and examine it. Look first for goals that are not likely within your power to achieve. From the list above we were able to tag items 6 and 8 as low probability items—virtually impossible to achieve. Spending much time attempting to achieve these goals is not cost effective. It would be like betting a large sum of money on a million-to-one shot. Goals like a tennis victory over Jimmy Connors, however, can be changed to achievable ones, such as improving your tennis game. If modifying the goal to make it achievable turns it into something you no longer care about, then drop the goal altogether.

Try to be clear about what you mean by each goal statement. The clearer and less general you can make a goal, the easier it is to decide whether the goal is reachable, and if it is reachable, how you would go about achieving it. For example, when our client got very specific about goal 10, it turned out that goal 10 meant being liked by "just about everybody."

Look for inconsistencies among your goals. Working toward incompatible goals can tear you apart psychologically. Examples of some common pairs of goals that are inconsistent in all but the rarest cases are the following:

1. Share the responsibility for housework and still have things done your way.
2. Rise to the top of your profession and never work weekends or evenings.
3. Do only work that really interests you and also earn a great deal of money.
4. Have children and also a great deal of freedom.
5. Have strong opinions, speak your mind, and still have everyone like you.

Nobody can function effectively when attempting to move simultaneously in opposite directions. Finding that goals are incompatible may cause you to drop one or more from your list or deemphasize the importance of some goals. At the very least, spotting conflicting goals will alert you to potential problems.

Rank-order the goals. Decide which goals are most important to you. Note also those goals that must be achieved, e.g., an income adequate to provide food and housing. Once you have analyzed and refined your list of goals, you are ready to derive a set of objectives for each of your goals. Objectives are specific, concrete outcomes that further your progress toward a goal. A statement of an objective must always refer to some publicly observable outcome occurring within a certain time frame. An objective is always stated in terms that allow outside observers to decide whether it has been achieved.

The statement "I'm going to get my finances better organized" is not a well-stated objective. It is an acceptable goal statement but is too vague to be an objective. A well-stated objective for the goal of financial organization would be, "By the fifth of this month, all outstanding bills will be paid and my checkbook will be up to date."

Objectives perform an important service. They enable us to break up the larger and more unwieldy goals into smaller, more manageable pieces. They also help us keep tabs on our progress. Perhaps most important of all, they are a safeguard against doing nothing more than paving the way to hell with good intentions.

Once you have precise, clear objectives you will be ready to select activities for the achievement of each objective. Well-stated objectives often suggest the activities necessary to accomplish them. Activities are the specific behaviors that lead to achieving objectives, which, in turn, means progress toward the goal. Good activities are those that provide a straightforward path toward the achievement of the objective. The activity of check writing is appropriate to the objective of getting the bills paid. Reading a book on balancing the family budget, while related to the matter at hand, does not pay the bills. Choosing activities that are related, but nonessential, to objectives is a common method of procrastination. We will discuss procrastination in a later section.

B. *Schedule Yourself and Record Your Behavior:* Purchase an appointment book, the kind that breaks up the day into half-hour blocks. Decide every week which of your goals you wish to pursue. Then pick an objective and activities related to that goal. Block out times for those activities and write them in your weekly schedule. Each night before you go to sleep, review the activities you have scheduled for the next day.

It is important that you keep a record of how faithfully you carry out each scheduled activity and your progress toward your objectives. You can enter this kind of record in your appointment book. At the end of each day when you are reviewing tomorrow's schedule, note whether you kept to your schedule and how effectively you performed each activity. (Use your own adjectives when describing your progress. Stay away from letter grades or numerical rankings.) Decide also how much activity remains to be performed before the objective is reached. This review process will help you make any necessary revisions in your schedule on a daily basis.

Scheduling can be an effective tool to reduce the hurrying and scurrying that most of us do. For example, much of the urgency and rushing in our lives can be reduced simply by scheduling a little extra time for activities. Try getting up a half-hour earlier one morning (even if you must retire earlier). That morning take your time. Eat breakfast slowly. Leave for work earlier. Soak up the sights and sounds along the way. Go slowly. Do not rush. Arrive at work earlier. Take a few minutes to daydream pleasantly or to organize your thoughts for the day.

One thing that scheduling does not imply is becoming obsessive about time. Far from making us slaves to the clock, scheduling turns time into an ally. Use scheduling to help you use time effectively. Give yourself a reasonable margin of error (up to fifteen minutes) for any appointment. And do not rush. By slowing down you may help make yourself late for the one appointment we would all like to postpone.

C. *Learn to Stop Procrastinating:* Procrastination, or putting off things that you want or need to do, goes hand in hand with stress. Procrastination usually involves trading tomorrow for today. Put another way, when we procrastinate we usually choose some activity that is immediately pleasant, such as watching television, over some other activity, such as doing homework, which is immediately less pleasant but whose completion would bring more longterm satisfaction. The benefits of such a choice are usually illusory. It would be one thing if we could gain total relief from our longterm commitments, but we generally cannot. They hang over our heads like the proverbial sword of Damocles, nagging at us, waiting to be done. Avoiding the work we have decided we will do is seldom a good idea. For the more we avoid the work the more likely we are to continue avoiding it. Ultimately avoidance breeds more avoidance. Avoiders fall farther and farther behind. The work mounts up and becomes still harder to tackle. There are methods for breaking this vicious circle. All of the methods involve attacking the factors that aid and abet procrastination:

1. *Perfectionism:* We have encountered this nemesis in earlier discusions. It lies at the root of many problems, including procrastination. Being a perfectionist makes one more likely also to be a procrastinator. This is because the more aversive a situation is, the more likely we are to avoid it. If you are a perfectionist, you are dissatisfied unless you do things perfectly. You always feel something of a failure if any performance has a flaw. Therefore, any task becomes aversive, because no job is ever done 100 percent right. Avoidance is a defense against the unpleasant struggle to be perfect and the inevitable failure of that struggle. The student who cannot get beyond the first page of a term paper because he just cannot stop crossing out sentences that are not of A quality is a good example of perfectionism in action. After some futile hours the student will avoid writing altogether until the night before the paper is due. By then it will be too late to produce the caliber of work he is capable of.

2. *Inappropriate Commitments:* People who have trouble accomplishing the work that is really important to them often say that they are so occupied with busy work that they cannot find the time to do the really important work. In order to do those things in life that are really important to you, you must learn to make appropriate commitments. Most of us are more likely to honor a commitment made to another person than we are to honor a commitment made to ourselves. This is a fact we can turn either to our advantage or disadvantage.

If you are the kind of person who says "Yes" to most requests made on your time by other people, you are likely someone who often does not get around to doing the things that are important to you. In order to be an effective achiever of your goals you must learn to make commitments to others that further your goals, and avoid commitments that only squander your time in the service of goals that are unimportant to you. Learning to screen out and say "No" to people who waste your time is a large part of having the time to do what you want to do. Conversely, making a commitment (especially a public commitment) to do something that is important to you is an excellent way to mobilize yourself. In writing this book our commitments to each other were often the only thing that made the difference between our writing and avoiding writing.

Behavior therapists have long known that individuals will usually get started on even the most arduous of tasks rather than face a significant penalty (such as the loss of money). You can demonstrate for yourself the power of this kind of commitment. The next time you find yourself procrastinating on a difficult but important job, deposit $100 with a friend or family member. Tell her that if the job is not fully completed (and give specific guidelines so there will be no disagreement) in a specified time, she is to burn the money. Unless you are very wealthy, the job will be done.

3. *Self-Deception:* There are two ways to procrastinate, the straightforward way and the deceptive way. Straightforward procrastination is going to a ball game when you need to be figuring your income tax. Devious procrastination involves performing some activity other than the target activity because it (1) is redeeming in some way, or (2) is "preparation" for the target activity. Reading a book entitled *Your Family Budget* when you need to pay your bills may not seem like avoidance, but it is avoidance, pure and simple. Under certain circumstances reading such a book may be a valuable activity, but in this case it is probably a device to obscure the fact that you are avoiding your work and to protect yourself from feeling guilty about it. When there is work to be done, you are either working or not working. Watching a television program to "relax" so you can later work is a feeble excuse for avoiding work and no real help in getting started. Deciding that it is time to get interested in some "good literature" just before you need to prepare a sales report may make you feel better while

you are procrastinating, but it will not help you get the work done any faster. Once you have set your priorities, either work or do not work. Learning to correctly label activities as avoidance is an important step in overcoming procrastination.

4. *Jobs That Are Too Big:* We often avoid getting to work on a project because it seems to be too big to tackle. For example, the idea of going around the world on a vacation seems for most of us not only an expensive but massively effortful kind of undertaking. This is because we think of it as a whole, undifferentiated endeavor, "going around the world." If we break the trip down into its constituent parts, it instantly becomes more manageable. First, we get passports. Then we arrange two weeks off from work. Next, we decide which places we would like to see. We then consult a travel agent to plan an itinerary and purchase tickets. Perhaps some vaccinations are necessary. Soon we are off.

The Chinese have a saying that a journey of a thousand miles begins with a single step. So, too, all undertakings, no matter how large, are comprised of component parts that usually can be tackled one at a time. For any goal there are smaller, more specific objectives and activities that can be designed to achieve those objectives. The next time a job seems too big to start, try breaking it up into component objectives and activities. Start on one activity, even if you only spend a very few minutes on it initially. You will be surprised at how much you are able to accomplish.

D. *Learn to Play:* For many of us, learning how to play is the most difficult of all objectives. The workaholic who can never be totally free of her job, or the person so wrapped up in the responsibilities of parenthood that he can never have time to himself, are people who need to learn how to goof off. The unrelenting pressures of job or family are dealt with much more effectively by people who can learn how to get away from them. The person who is not able to play is usually irritable, depressed, or anxious. He has little fun and is never an effective or efficient worker.

Sometimes people play too little because of poor planning or scheduling or because they have procrastinated too long, leaving no time for play. Learning to work more efficiently, using the methods described earlier, will make it easier to find time that you will feel good about using for play. For those of us who lead very busy lives, play time may have to be planned for and scheduled, as any other activity. Some people use play time to "reward" themselves after some accomplishment. This kind of self-reinforcement can often not only help you get more work done, but can also result in more time spent playing. But in no sense can all play be thought of as a bonus or a luxury. Play is a necessity. Make sure you spend a reasonable portion of your life doing things that get you away from your duties and responsibilities.

Changing our behavior, as well as changing our thinking, can reduce stress. The four cornerstones of such an approach are planning, scheduling and record keeping, overcoming procrastination, and play. Improving your performance in any one of these areas can enable you to function more effectively and thereby lower stress. Making improvements in all four areas can greatly improve your chances to minimize the stress in your life.

resolving
interpersonal
conflicts

Susan felt rotten. The argument with Dave had been so pointless. Nothing was ever settled in these fights. Sometimes she thought it would be better to keep her mouth shut, but at times she just could not hold back. Since she had gone back to work the load had been unbearable. She had what amounted to two fulltime jobs. Despite their many conversations about everybody's pitching in, Dave and the kids were pretty unreliable. The housework seemed inevitably to fall back on Susan. At her job her responsibilities were increasing. She was eager for a promotion and wished that she had more energy to put into her work. But the fighting left her drained and depleted. All aspects of her relationship with Dave had deteriorated. It seemed to her as though she must work twice as hard with only half the energy she used to have.

Conflict between ourselves and other persons undoubtedly produces much of the most debilitating stress that we experience. Marital discord, job dissatisfaction, and the inability to maintain rewarding friendships very often stem directly from the failure to deal effectively with conflict. Learning how to resolve conflicts constructively is an important asset to anyone attempting to lower the stress in his or her life. But before we begin our discussion of conflict resolution, we must define a few terms. In so doing we will draw heavily from the psychologist Marton Deutsch.

First of all, the term *conflict,* as we shall use it, is not synonymous with fighting or arguing. Two people can be in conflict without an open outbreak of hostilities. Two people are in conflict when at least one of them thinks there is an incompatibility between them with respect to some issue, goal, or action. Conflict is an inescapable part of living. The enormous diversity of backgrounds, tastes, and dispositions among people makes conflict inevitable. Generally speaking, the more significant and intimate the relationship, the greater the opportunities for conflict. We cannot make conflict disappear. Nor would it be desirable if we could. For without conflict life would be homogeneous, sterile, and boring. Conflict can be healthy, stimulating, and constructive. The more usual pattern, however, is one of hostility and destructiveness. To understand the processes of constructive vs. destructive conflict resolution we first must examine the concepts of competition and cooperation.

Competitive situations are those in which the individuals involved see it as a win-lose situation. If one person wins the other must lose, and vice versa. A footrace is an example of an inescapably competitive situation. There can be only one winner and if you are a runner, then the success of anyone else in the race is by definition your failure.

Cooperative situations, on the other hand, are those in which each person assumes she will be benefited when other people get what they want. Rather than diminishing the fortunes of other people, each person's success actually promotes the success of the other. The people therefore tend to conceive of themselves as members of the same team. If the footrace cited above is a relay race, then the situation is competitive between teams but cooperative within teams.

Conflicts always occur within social systems, and these systems are of two kinds: open and closed. Whether a system is open or closed in large measure determines the methods of conflict resolution that will be effective within that system. A closed system is one in which the relationships are regular, ongoing, and interdependent. In closed systems people's fortunes are tied together and actions of one member are likely to have significant effects on other members of the system. A family is an example of a closed system. So is an office staff. An open system is one in which no important interdependent relationships exist. The people within an open system are much less important to each other and have less influence over each others' lives. You and a stranger you speak briefly with on a bus (and will never see again) could be said to constitute an extremely open system. If you argue with this stranger, the argument will end with the bus ride. You and the stranger will carry any residual irritation away with you into your separate, unrelated lives.

Conflict often creates ill will, hurt feelings, resentment, anxiety, depression, and bitterness. Open systems are those that allow these forms of psychological pollution to escape, primarily affecting people outside the system. In closed systems the poisonous aftermath of conflict remains within the system and affects all members of the system. In closed systems it is impossible to win an argument or be on top in a relationship. This is because in a closed system the feelings and actions of one person always influence the feelings of every other member of the system. If my wife "wins" the argument over where we will spend our vacation, she really loses because if one spouse loses, both lose. She may have her choice of holiday sites, but her fun may very well be spoiled by the lack of enthusiasm of her partner. Even if the vacation goes relatively well, she will probably suffer in some way because of her victory. We usually pay dearly for victories won over those whose fortunes are tied to ours. In situations where the good will between parties is secondary or unimportant, we can confront, demand, and assert to get our way. However, the cost of such an aggressive strategy in longterm relationships is very great.

Methods of Resolving Conflicts
Being Assertive

The popularity of such books as *When I Say No I Feel Guilty* and *Your Perfect Right* have made *assertive* a house-bold word. Assertiveness-training courses are springing up all over. These courses teach people to stand up for their rights and to avoid being pushed around by other people. The premise of assertiveness-training is that when you come into conflict with other people it is best to speak out in a reasonable and balanced fashion, making it clear what you desire and expect out of a situation. The assumption is that we can reduce our overall level of anxiety about social situations if we can learn to assert ourselves. A further assumption is that very often in an interpersonal conflict, one person will come out with the short end of the stick. Presumably, if you learn to be assertive, that loser will not be you.

The appropriateness of assertive behavior depends, in large measure, on whether the relationship is a casual one or is more intimate. Confronting a stranger in a store over which of the two of you had the right to be waited on next is an entirely different matter from standing up to your spouse over who has the right to decide where the family will take a vacation. In the first case one may bolster one's self-esteem, overcome some social anxiety, and save some time by being assertive. In the second instance demanding one's rights is a sure prescription for disaster. Remember that in closed systems one often wins a battle only to lose the war.

The general principle to be gleaned from the preceding discussion is that, from your point of view, the way you choose to resolve conflicts will depend on the situation you find yourself in. If you find what you consider to be your legitimate rights being infringed upon by a person with whom you are intimately involved, you may not be able to lower the stress in your life by "winning" the point. With people you live with, with people whose moods will inevitably affect your moods, you need a solution that both of you can live with.

Issue Identification

The first step in attempting to resolve any conflict is to decide what the conflict is about. More specifically, the answer is sought to the question: "What are the issues over which there is incompatibility and disagreement?" In many cases the answer to this question may seem obvious. If you and your spouse are in conflict over where you will take your summer vacation, it seems apparent that the central issue is the summer vacation. It is, unfortunately, not always that simple. A dispute between husband and wife over who will take out the garbage may, in fact, have more to do with a conflict over who is to wield power within the family or what roles husband and wife are to play.

It is often difficult to tell whether the issue on the surface or some less obvious, less easily defined issue is what really is at stake. There are two general indications that some unexpressed issue may be the real source of the disagreement:

1. Repeated conflicts centering around issues with a common theme.
2. Continuation of conflict after the surface issue is resolved.

We often find antagonism within relationships in the absence of what appear to be clear issues. Angry exchanges between people often develop suddenly, seeming to have no cause other than one person's touchiness. Take the example of the man married to a championship tennis player. His game, while respectable, is levels below his wife's. They are playing as partners in a doubles match. After her husband has missed several shots at the net, giving their opponents a large lead, the wife says to her husband, "You'd better back up behind the baseline." His response, "Don't tell me what to do," is spoken angrily. An argument ensues.

What is the issue involved in this disagreement? A likely candidate is differing views about sex roles and marital roles. The husband may believe, at some level, that it is a degradation of himself to be inferior to a woman in athletics. He probably feels that wives should not instruct their husbands on the subject of athletics, especially in public. His wife, on the other hand, may see her husband in this context as just another tennis partner who should not be offended at the demonstration of her superior skill and knowledge. These are issues that need to be resolved before they will be a compatible doubles team.

At least one identifiable issue is almost always central to every interpersonal conflict. Learning to recognize the issues central to a conflict requires practice, but it is a skill that can be learned. When you look for the issues causing the conflicts in your life, keep in mind the following categories. These are the kinds of issues that are most often at the source of conflict.

1. *Matters of fact.* An example of this would be two friends disagreeing over the shortest route to some destination.

2. *Values.* A husband and wife would be in conflict over values if he believes that religious training is desirable for children while she is opposed to all organized religion.

3. *Personal space.* Here an example would be an office worker who brings a radio to the office, and plays it loud enough that his coworker is disturbed by the noise.

4. *Rewards.* Rewards are things or experiences that people will seek out or work for. Two friends disagreeing over which of two movies to see would be an example of this kind of conflict.

5. *Roles.* A conflict over roles would exist if a wife wanted her husband to share in the housework but this violated his conception of appropriate masculine behavior.

The Art of Compromise: learning
to be more satisfied with less

Once the issues are identified and the positions on the issues are clear, one can begin the process of resolving the conflicts. All the methods that we will describe are based on the concept of compromise. In the kind of closed system relationship in which both parties must be satisfied for either to achieve longterm satisfaction, compromise is the only answer. Any true victory must be the victory of the relationship over competitiveness and excessive self-centeredness. We assume that each relationship is unique, that there are no magic formulas to tell people how to behave in all relationships. It is our experience that in most relationships the people must come to an understanding that works for them. What follows are general guidelines and some specific techniques that can help you be more effective in working out the unique set of rules and agreements that will best serve each of your significant relationships. We suggest that before attempting any of the suggestions offered you might consider giving the other individual involved the opportunity to read and become familiar with the ideas presented in this chapter.

1. *Establishment of trust and cooperative norms of conduct.* The best way to achieve trust and cooperation is to change your own competitive orientation. If you are out for yourself, exclusively, it forces others to become competitive in order to protect themselves. Another way to encourage trust is to make a clean breast of your wishes and intentions. Telling the truth is the best way to be believed. This is not a directive to compulsively disclose anything and everything to the people who are close to you. But when you want something, it is generally best to admit that you want it rather than to choose a deceptive route to your goal. Remember that the establishment of trust in a relationship is usually more important than getting some one thing that you want. You can also work to establish cooperative norms by choosing, whenever possible, an approach of compromise and cooperation. If you behave cooperatively and practice what you preach it is more likely the other person will also behave cooperatively. For example, if you wish to see one movie and a friend prefers to see another, you can foster trust and cooperation by saying, "I would really like to see film A and don't want to see film B. But let's not do something that one of us doesn't wish to. Perhaps there is a third film we would both like to see or some other thing we could do."

2. *Issue Control.* This has to do with learning to define issues in ways that will aid the productive resolution of conflict. For example, suppose a wife complains to her husband that he is no longer attentive to her and probably does not love her. The husband may contend that his love for his wife is as great as it has ever been. It is always difficult to settle a dispute over who loves whom how much. The larger, the less tangible, and the more sensitive an issue, the more difficult it is to resolve a conflict that is defined in terms of that issue. In our example, however, the issue of attentiveness is much easier to grapple with. To the wife, attentiveness probably

means specific acts, such as compliments, invitations to go out, and sexual advances. Usually people can agree about whether these kinds of events have occurred and discuss the possibility of increasing them. Choosing to talk about specific acts of attention rather than the more global construct of "love" separates a smaller, more resolvable issue from a larger, less resolvable one. This is almost always a useful process, especially in marriage, where small issues often take on larger, more symbolic meaning.

2. *Tradeoffs.* One of the basic ingredients of compromises and other quasi-contractual agreements is that of a *quid pro quo*. As it applies to relationships the notion of *quid pro quo* implies that in any successful agreement between two individuals there must be payoffs for both people. Otherwise the agreement is less satisfying to both parties and consequently less likely to be honored. Agreements that are too one-sided always leave one person feeling exploited and often resentful. If you want someone to increase some desired behavior or to decrease some behavior you do not like, you are well advised to make it worth that person's while to change. This will show the person that the change you asked for was important to you. It will also make the other person feel that you are concerned with more than just your own convenience. If you would like your husband to start doing more of the housework, do not assume that he should help, even though this, in fact, may be a good idea. Think rather in terms of what you might do that would similarly improve the quality of his life. If you want your wife to start paying the bills, there is undoubtedly something you can do for her to make paying the bills a worthwhile effort for her. If you and a friend both dislike driving to the bowling alley, you can alternate the times that you drive.

Some people are repelled by the suggestion that one might introduce bargaining and the language of the marketplace into such an intimate relationship as marriage. To these critics we reply that we are suggesting alternatives to *destructive conflict*, not to those aspects of a relationship that are already functioning satisfactorily.

Often the payoffs to each member of a relationship are adequate without there being the need for explicit negotiation. Even in the best of relationships, however, conflicts of interest do arise. In these instances we favor openness, cooperation, reason, and compromise over the deception, competition, irrationality, and schisms that usually characterize interpersonal conflict.

4. *Relaxation.* One of the factors that aggravates the destructiveness of conflict is arousal. When we are in conflict with another we become emotionally aroused. When we are excessively emotional we become preoccupied with our own personal positions and less able to understand the other's point of view. We also become more defensive and less able to think clearly. All of these changes make us likely to say, think, and do things that will intensify the conflict.

Using one of the relaxation methods described in Chapters 10, 11, and 12, you can learn to lower your level of arousal in a matter of seconds. After you have learned how to do this, try relaxing yourself the next time you find yourself in a conflict situation. If you can, leave the situation for a few minutes, go into another room, sit down, close your eyes, and relax. You will return to the situation better able to cope with it. If you cannot leave the situation, it is still possible to lower your level of arousal while remaining in the situation by using a modification of the self-hypnosis method, relaxation by recall, or conditioned relaxation technique described in later chapters.

5. *Deattribution.* In Chapter 3, "Stress and Anger," we spoke of the attribution process and how we have a tendency to see ourselves as responding justifiably to the demands of the situation while seeing the behavior of others as arising out of their intentions or out of the kind of people they are, rather than out of the kind of situation they find themselves in. In conflict situations this tendency is exaggerated, causing us to focus on the other person as the cause of the conflict, while we see ourselves as only responding out of necessity to the actions of the other. We are thus more likely to see the other person as attacking, instigating, and causing, while

we see ourselves as defending, reacting, and being affected. The perspective of the other person is, of course, exactly reversed. He sees himself as the good guy who is only holding his ground against attack. This difference in perspective, which causes us to see the other as responding out of a different set of causes from the ones we are reacting to, makes it difficult to either trust him or empathize with him. We are more likely to blame him, label him, and accuse him. This, in turn, makes communication less open and effective. All of these factors serve to worsen and intensify conflict.

One method of counteracting these tendencies in ourselves is to program ourselves to be more rational in understanding the perspective of the other person in a conflict. To achieve this, we begin by teaching our clients conditioned relaxation (see Chapter 11). When they have mastered this technique, they are able to bring on relaxation by taking a deep breath and saying the word *relax* to themselves as they slowly exhale. We then have them practice quickly bringing on relaxation in this fashion while pairing the relaxation with the following speech (silently spoken just after the exhalation is complete):

> The other person is just as bothered as I am— maybe just as threatened and uptight. His/her behavior seems to him/her to be an automatic and justified response to my behavior, just as my behavior seems to me to be only a natural reaction to his/her behavior. I can only improve things by making a constructive response.

If one practices this exercise several times per day it causes an association to be formed between relaxation and this empathetic and rational view of the other person's perspective. When you find yourself in a conflict situation relax yourself, using conditioned relaxation. In addition to deriving the benefits of relaxation alluded to in the previous section, the relaxation will cue you to recall the reprogramming message, which in turn will help you to counteract the destructive effects of the attributional process.

6. *Role reversal.* Role reversal involves a bit of play-acting in which you and another person switch roles for a brief period of time. You and your partner each attempt to portray the motives, beliefs, and feelings of the other as you honestly believe them to be. To use role reversal you and your partner must find a room free from distractions, where you will not be disturbed. Pick an issue on which you disagree. Now give your partner five minutes to present his side of the issue. This should be a five-minute monologue. No interruptions! After your partner is finished, assume his role and present his viewpoint as if you were he. Now without any discussion, immediately present your own feelings and thoughts on the conflict for five minutes, subsequently giving your partner five minutes to reverse roles. After you and your partner have each presented both sides, you may spend some time discussing discrepancies in the portrayals. In this discussion the objective is, in good faith, to attempt to resolve differences in how you perceive yourself and how you are perceived by the other person. This is not a time to take shots at each other. This technique offers several advantages. It gets you "off your own trip" for a while, perhaps enabling your position to become more flexible. It forces you to try to understand the other person's position. It shows you what the other person perceives your position to be. It enables both of you to correct misconceptions about what your feelings and intentions are. Our clients report that this technique not only helps them discover what the relevant issues and feelings are, but that it also makes them more sensitive and tolerant toward the other person.

The methods of conflict resolution presented in this chapter have proven effective for many individuals. You should not expect, however, quick and easy success in learning how to handle interpersonal conflict more effectively. Part of the difficulty lies in the fact that when conflict exists, both sides must desire peace in order for there to be peace. Because cooperation is by definition a joint venture, it is not completely within your power to make your interpersonal relationships cooperative. This chapter, however, can be a beginning step in that direction. Understanding more about the nature of conflict is a help in learning how to resolve conflicts more effectively. The methods provided in this chapter can be helpful in changing destructive patterns of conflict into constructive means of resolving disagreements. As such they can play an important role in your program of stress reduction.

10

meditation

In recent years a method of combating stress that has received wide publicity is meditation. Before the advent of the Maharishi Mahesh Yogi and his famous disciples, however, the practice of meditation was relatively uncommon in the Western world. Today there are in excess of a million individuals who have been trained in Transcendental Meditation and various other meditative techniques. Because of extravagant claims about the benefits of meditation, and because it has long been associated with Eastern mystical practices, many have looked upon it with some suspicion. This skepticism is healthy when applied to teachers or groups claiming the ultimate superiority or greater legitimacy of their approaches. For recent research by scientists intent on taking the mystery out of meditation has indicated that several methods of meditation are effective in reducing arousal and producing feelings of inner calm. Furthermore, it is likely that the various methods that are effective, are effective for the same reasons. In this chapter we will discuss the scientifically documented benefits of meditation, enumerate the common features of the various methods, and provide the reader with an easily learned meditation technique that he himself can practice and thereby derive the stress-reducing benefits.

What can meditation actually do for members of stressful, high-speed Western societies? Much research suggests that meditation can, at least for some people, reduce the amount of stress they experience. When measurements are taken during meditation the pattern that emerges is one of generally lowered physiological arousal. Oxygen consumption and respiration decrease, the ability of the skin to conduct electrical current (a measure of arousal) decreases and stabilizes, and brain waves show a pattern of slow, synchronized activity. Wallace and Benson called this meditative state hypometabolic, meaning that during meditation the metabolism of the body becomes slower and more quiescent. This is a pattern that is physiologically opposite to that of the fight-or-flight response. Meditation appears to produce deep physiological relaxation and feelings of peace and tranquility. The meditative state, however, is not similar to being asleep or chemically tranquilized. Meditation involves an active process of attention focusing, and although it reduces arousal, it leaves mental alertness undiminished.

Some writers have assumed that the practice of meditation operates as a kind of general desensitization procedure that tunes our autonomic nervous systems to be less easily aroused by stress. At the very least meditation can give the mind a rest—a brief vacation from stress and worry, one that requires neither a travel agent nor days free from the responsibilities of work or family. When focusing all attention upon a mantra or meditative object one cannot simultaneously be paying attention to stressful events or thoughts. Thus successful meditation requires that one take some time and attention away from the hassles of daily life. Meditators often report themselves to feel refreshed and invigorated following meditation. It is almost as though meditation allows us to temporarily shut down those information-processing mechanisms of the brain that are ultimately responsible for producing stress. This short vacation from stress rests and revitalizes our coping abilities, giving us a more balanced outlook and increased energy for dealing with whatever difficulties we are faced with. Interrupting a fruitless, emotion-generating train of thought by interposing a relaxing activity such as meditation can result in diminished stress both during the period of meditation and after it is over. We have all had the experience of having taken a break from some aversive activity only to find that, upon returning, the situation was not so bad as we initially had believed. It is as though an anxious or angry perspective is disrupted and altered not only by the cooling off and increased sense of peace that results from meditation, but also simply by the passage of some time during which the fires of arousal are not actively fueled by emotion-laden thoughts.

Some recent research in England attempted to investigate the hypothesis that individuals who practice meditation would show less reaction to stressful stimulation than a group of matched control subjects. All subjects were placed in a laboratory and exposed to loud, noxious sounds. The meditators showed significantly less arousal than did the group of non-meditators. In yet another study meditators and nonmeditators were shown a film depicting grisly woodshop accidents. This film has been used as a stimulus in much research on stress and never fails to generate heightened arousal in those who view it. Both the physiological records and the reports of the subjects indicated that the meditators tolerated the film with less stress than did the control group. A novel feature of this experiment was the inclusion of some subjects who meditated for the first time during the study. Even among these individuals it was found that meditation reduced the stress of viewing the film. These data and the results of other investigations suggest that meditators may develop some degree of immunity to stress.

The apparent effectiveness of meditation as an antidote to stress certainly makes it a desirable component in a comprehensive program for the reduction of stress. Meditative techniques are generally simple and easy to learn. Virtually all forms of meditation share three common features. These common elements involve assuming a comfortable body position, maintaining physical immobility, and continuously focusing attention on some object, sound, or bodily process. Do these things and, by definition, you are meditating.

If this all sounds too easy to you, that is because the real difficulty in meditation comes not with initiating the operations involved but with maintaining them. In other words, meditation is easy to learn but somewhat difficult to practice. There are reasons for this.

First of all, meditation requires one to sit quietly and engage in simple, monotonous activity. To most Westerners meditation instructions sound like a prescription for boredom rather than either relaxation or enlightenment. For many of us it is hard to accept the idea of spending time doing virtually nothing. Of course doing "virtually nothing" is the whole point of meditation and the process from which most of its benefits derive. But this is a kind of pastime foreign to the majority of us and one which we are prejudiced against. The fact that many Westerners have learned to find the process of meditation pleasurable and soothing is evidence that we can adapt ourselves to this pursuit. But before beginning to attempt meditation, the reader should understand that he will likely find that he will not take to it immediately, but will probably have to develop a taste for it.

Another related problem that many people have with meditation is in adopting the necessary attitude of passive attention. This is again a psychological *modus operandi* with which most Westerners are unfamiliar. We typically conceive of our activities as "trying to do something." In meditation the expending of too much active effort defeats the purpose. While meditating, one is not actively striving, but rather allowing herself to "flow with" or "be with" the object of meditation. Think of the times you have found yourself totally absorbed in a sensory experience such as listening to a beautiful piece of music or receiving a massage. At that time you were unlikely to be either analyzing your experience or attempting to manipulate it. This kind of psychological posture is very similar to that required in meditation.

A third problem that people have in learning to meditate is self-evaluation. We all like to feel that whatever we do we do well. Many people will not even attempt activities at which they feel they cannot excel. However, the lexicon of success and failure does not apply to meditation. One does not meditate "well" or "poorly." If one is attending to the object of meditation, one is meditating. If one's attention is not focused upon the object of meditation, then one is not meditating. Meditation is, by definition, value-free. One simply is either meditating or not meditating. It is, therefore, self-defeating to try to do well while meditating. The chances are that if someone is trying to meditate well, then she will be thinking about how well she is doing rather than maintaining her focus on the object of meditation. Trying to meditate well will therefore keep one from meditating at all.

The proper attutide toward meditation does not come naturally to many of us. One can, however, attempt to approximate this attitude when beginning to practice meditation. The following are some additional guidelines which, if adhered to, will make it possible for the reader to derive maximum benefits from the practice of meditation. When meditating:

1. Limit the sensory stimulation in the environment. Choose a quiet room. If none is available, use acoustical ear plugs or put some cotton in your ears. Dim the lights. Keep your eyes closed during meditation. Arrange for others to understand that you are not to be bothered while meditating. Please, no telephones, radios, or televisions!

2. Sit in a comfortable position, one which does not restrict your breathing. Unless you are experienced in assuming Yoga asanas (postures), it is a good idea to provide your back with support. The essential requirement is to sit in a position that can be comfortably maintained for twenty minutes. Physical discomfort is distracting, and distraction is the enemy of meditation.

3. Wear comfortable clothes. Clothing should be loose and unrestricting. It is desirable but not essential to loosen ties, belts, and foundation garments and to remove shoes, eyeglasses, and contact lenses.

4. Meditate two times per day for fifteen minutes at a stretch. For many persons this is the most difficult to follow of all the guidelines. The question we often receive is "Do I have to stick to two fifteen-minute sessions a day for meditation to help me?" Research provides no clear answer to this question but it is likely that some meditation, any meditation, is better than none. We have evidence from our clinical work and reports from our colleagues that many people have been able to reduce

the stress in their lives by following a variety of meditation patterns. Meditating once a day for thirty minutes or three times a day for five minutes can be helpful. Probably the most important consideration is finding the pattern of meditation that disrupts your life the least. For this is the schedule you will be most likely to stay with. And meditation, like physical exercise, is of value only if one does it.

What follows is a set of instructions that we employ in the teaching of meditation. This method incorporates features from both Zen meditation (Zazen) and from Yoga. We suggest that you read the instructions and then immediately practice the technique for about five minutes before reading on.

You will soon be learning an uncomplicated but very effective method of concentration and relaxation. Inability to reduce stress is associated with an inability to stop thinking the thoughts that produce stress. The ability to turn off stressful thoughts and to focus upon something other than troubling sensations and feelings is an important aid in learning to reduce stress. The technique you will be learning is a skill. As in the case of any skill, if you are to become accomplished, you must practice it regularly.

Begin by getting as comfortable as you can. Close your eyes. Let your breathing become relaxed and natural. Allow it to find its own rhythm and depth. Now focus your attention on your breathing: the movements of your chest and stomach, not those of your nose and throat. Don't allow any thought or stimulus to pull your attention away from your breathing. Focus your entire awareness upon your breathing. This may be hard to do at first. Thoughts, sensations, sounds may distract you temporarily. That's O.K. That's to be expected. As soon as you are aware that your attention has wandered, just bring it back to your breathing.

In order to help you regulate your attention, we want you silently to say two words to yourself while you are breathing. The words are *in* and *out*. As you inhale, say the word *in* to yourself. As you exhale, say the word *out* to yourself. We want you to say these words in a special way. Extend or draw out the pronunciation of each word, so that during the entire time you are inhaling, you are saying the word *in*, and the entire time you are exhaling, you are saying the word *out*. If you are breathing slowly, it might sound like this:

i-i-i-i-i-i-i-n-n-n-n-n-n————ow-ow-ow-ow-t-t-t-t-t

This means that at all times you will be saying one of these two words. Just as it is practically impossible to say aloud two different words at the same time, it is practically impossible to think two different thoughts at the same time. If all your attention is focused on your breathing, and you are saying these words *in* and *out* silently, you'll find that other thoughts can't occur. Freedom from distracting thoughts may not come quickly, but don't concern yourself. Just return your attention to your breathing and resume saying *in* and *out*.

A word of explanation. When we say focus your attention on your breathing, we don't mean we want you to evaluate the depth or pace, or explain, or think about your breathing in any way. Just go with it, let it happen, don't try to push it or control it. Don't fill your mind with evaluations of how well you are doing; then you are not totally concentrating, and the *in* and the *out* are not the only words you are saying to yourself. Remember, the idea is not to try to achieve anything. The idea is to concentrate, nothing more—nothing less. As soon as you wander from this total focus, don't put yourself down, just resume concentrating on your breathing and saying the words *in* and *out*.

If you are not experienced in meditation, you probably found that you were often distracted from the mantra and your breathing. We suggest that you reread the preceding pages of this chapter before attempting another meditation session. Remember the appropriate attitude and remember that it often takes some time to develop an affinity for meditation.

It is possible that after some time spent using the previously described technique, you may wish to experiment with some variations of method. There are several that we can recommend:

1. Change the mantra. You might choose a traditional Sanskrit word such as *om* or *ram*. Any other sound that feels right to you is appropriate.

2. Experiment with exercising less control over the manner in which you silently utter the mantra. In other words, each time you say the mantra you can vary the time it takes to say it, as well as the volume, pitch, and melodiousness of the mantra. If you choose this variation, drop the focus of breathing. Direct all attention to the mantra.

3. Instead of meditating with eyes closed, open your eyes and gaze at a vase, flower, burning candle, or other visually soothing object. Here the aim would be to direct attention to the visual perception of the object rather than the bodily sensations arising from breathing. This meditation can be performed either with or without a mantra.

progressive relaxation

Of all the different means of achieving relaxation, none has received less publicity than progressive relaxation. Despite the relative obscurity of this method, progressive relaxation is perhaps the most reliable and effective procedure of all. This method is based on the relationship between muscle tension and psychological tension. For many years scientists have known that the tension within skeletal muscles increases when the body prepares to deal with an emergency. At one time this increase in muscle tension, which is an accompaniment of the fight-or-flight response, was an aid in the struggle for survival. Tense muscles form a shield that protects the vital organs of the body from injury. Furthermore, a moderate amount of tension in the muscles makes them more efficient, better able to execute rapid movements. Those of us who are not regularly engaged in physical combat, however, derive virtually no benefit from this tendency of our muscles to tense up when we are experiencing uptight emotions. Muscle tension is the cause of many headaches and backaches and plays a central role in producing emotional discomfort.

The research of Edmund Jacobson led him to conclude that not only did tense muscles and tense emotions go hand in hand, but that in a very real sense, tight, contracted muscles were at the root of much emotional distress. Jacobson believed that if one could find a way to completely relax the muscles, mental relaxation would inevitably follow. In the 1930s he found such a method. Jacobson's patients who learned his method of progressive relaxation were able to eliminate most tension from their muscles. Seemingly, the more relaxed their muscles became, the more relaxed they felt inside. Furthermore, Jacobson found progressive relaxation training to be an effective treatment for such diverse disorders as anxiety, ulcers, hypertension, and insomnia.

The original Jacobsonian method of progressive relaxation was extraordinarily lengthy. Approximately sixty hours of training were required and extensive attention was given to each of thirty-nine separate muscle groups. The training has been abbreviated over the years so that it is now possible to learn an effective method of progressive relaxation in a few weeks.

Research has shown that briefer versions of progressive relaxation are quite effective in alleviating the discomfort produced by stress. Gordon Paul and his associates at the University of Illinois conducted a series of studies that demonstrated that progressive relaxation reduces both physical arousal and psychological distress. One experiment showed that subjects who learned progressive relaxation were less adversely affected by imagining stressful scenes than a control group who tried to relax without benefit of training.

Paul M. Lehrer of Rutgers Medical School has recently found that even severely anxious individuals can benefit from progressive relaxation training. His study was conducted with patients whose anxiety symptoms were quite severe. After receiving training in progressive relaxation, these individuals evidenced both reduced physiological arousal and relief from feelings of inner turmoil.

Progressive relaxation, as we teach it, involves several basic features. Trainees initially are taught to tense a muscle group (such as a hand and forearm), to hold it tight for approximately seven seconds, and then to release the tension abruptly and completely. The effect of this procedure is to leave the muscles less contracted than at the start of the tension-release cycle. You can get a sense of what this experience is like by placing your right arm on a solid surface, making a tight fist with your right hand, counting to five, and then opening your fist and allowing your hand and arm to relax completely. Do this and focus your attention on the sensations of warmth and relaxation that develop in your hand and forearm during the twenty seconds or so immediately after the release of tension. If you learned nothing more than how to tense and release tension from each of the major muscle groups, you would have at your disposal an effective method of inducing deep relaxation. But progressive relaxation involves more than simply learning to relax your muscles. A large part of the training is, in effect, body sensitivity training. While learning to tense and relax your muscles, you should pay careful attention to the way your muscles feel when they are tense as well as the feelings present during relaxation. By doing this you will greatly increase your sensitivity to the presence of tension in your muscles. Although rising muscle tension is a signal that we are under stress, most of us are unaware of it when our muscles begin to tighten. We usually become aware only when the tension reaches such high levels that we experience pain. Mounting tension in our muscles is often our first indication that stress is increasing. Learning to recognize this muscle tension early is a key step in eventually reducing stress.

One of the chief advantages that progressive relaxation has over the other methods presented in this book, meditation and self-hypnosis, is its relative obscurity. Since you likely have heard little or nothing of it before reading these pages, you probably have few fears or doubts about it.

Another advantage of progressive relaxation is that it is the least mental of the three techniques. Whereas a negative attitude toward hypnosis or meditation will usually render those methods ineffective, one can learn progressive relaxation without an open and receptive mind. If you follow instructions and learn to relax your muscles, you certainly will find yourself feeling more relaxed. Although progressive relaxation may be the method least affected by skepticism, receptiveness and motivation are, nevertheless, assets to speedy and effective learning.

Choosing conducive surroundings is a must for learning progressive relaxation. The following guidelines will be helpful to you in creating an appropriate physical environment for relaxation:

1. Find a quiet room where you will not be disturbed. Keep the lights dim and the distractions to a minimum.
2. Find a bed, couch, or overstuffed recliner. To learn progressive relaxation, all parts of your body must be supported comfortably. If any muscle is engaged in supporting you, it cannot relax. And, achieving muscle relaxation throughout your body is essential to learning this method.
3. Wear comfortable clothing. Avoid tight-fitting garments or undergarments. Remove shoes, eyeglasses, and contact lenses.

You are now ready to begin. Read the following description of how to produce tension in each of the muscle groups described below. Practice the movements until you can create tension in each area. You can experiment with modifying the instructions a bit to find the movement that best produces tension for you. It is important, however, that each tensing effort should produce tension only in the target region. At all times you should avoid retensing a muscle group after it has become relaxed.

1. *Right/left hand and forearm.* (Begin with your dominant side.) Make a very tight fist.
2. *Right/left upper arm.* Press your elbow down into the armrest of the chair. While pressing down, try to move your upper arm toward your rib cage.
3. *Left/right hand and forearm.* Same as 1.
4. *Left/right upper arm.* Same as 2.
5. *Forehead.* Raise your eyebrows as high as you can. If this movement does not produce tension, try making a deep frown.
6. *Middle face.* Wrinkle your nose and shut your eyelids tightly together.
7. *Jaws.* Clench your teeth and pull back the corners of

your mouth. At the same time press your tongue against the roof of your mouth.

8. *Neck.* Pull your chin toward your chest with the muscles in the front of your neck while simultaneously pulling your head back with the muscles in the rear of your neck.

9. *Shoulders and upper back.* Pull your shoulders back as though you were trying to touch your shoulder blades together. An alternative movement is to shrug your shoulders. Raise your shoulders as though you were trying to touch your ears with the tops of your shoulders.

10. *Stomach.* Pull the muscles of your stomach inward while at the same time pressing them downward. This makes your stomach hard, as you would if you were preparing to be hit in the stomach.

11. *Right/left thigh.* Try to bend your knee forward with the muscles of the back of your thigh while at the same time bending it in the opposite direction with the muscles on the top of your thigh.

12. *Right/left calf.* Bend your foot toward your shin as though you were trying to touch your shin with your toes. (Note that this is the opposite movement from pointing your toes.)

13. *Left/right thigh.* Same as 11.

14. *Left/right calf.* Same as 12.

Now that you can create tension in each of the fourteen muscle groups, you are ready to start relaxing. Read the relaxation instructions below several times. Then tape record the instructions. Then while sitting or reclining in an appropriate setting, play the recording. Close your eyes and keep them closed throughout the session. Follow each of the instructions as you hear yourself read it. (If a tape recorder is not available, you can have someone else read the instructions, or you may memorize the instructions and silently repeat them to yourself.)

Relaxation Instructions

Begin by making yourself as comfortable as you can. Settle back until you feel comfortable and completely supported. Now take a deep breath. Fill your lungs with air and hold your breath. (Pause for seven seconds.) Now let the breath out and let yourself begin to relax and let go of all the tension in your body. . . . Now direct your attention to the muscles of your right hand and forearm. At the signal, tense these muscles. TENSE. Hold that tension, study it, be aware of what tension feels like in these muscles and . . . (total of seven seconds) RELAX. Relax completely. When you relax after tension, let go immediately—not gradually. Now focus on the relaxation as it spreads into your arm and hand. Be aware of the difference between tension and relaxation as the muscles loosen and relax. Let yourself enjoy these pleasant sensations . . . (total of thirty to forty seconds after release). Now once again tense your right hand and forearm. TENSE. Focus on the tension . . . (total of seven seconds after TENSE) and RELAX. Once again notice the difference in feeling between tension and relaxation. Feel the pleasant sensations as the muscles loosen and relax . . . (total of forty-five to sixty seconds after RELAX). Now focus on the muscles of your right upper arm. At the signal tense these muscles. TENSE. Hold that tension, study it, be aware of what tension feels like in these muscles and . . . (total of seven seconds) RELAX. Relax completely. Now focus on the relaxation as it spreads into your upper arm. Be aware of the difference between tension and relaxation as the muscles loosen and relax. Let yourself enjoy these pleasant sensations . . . (total of thirty to forty seconds after release). Now once again tense your right upper arm. TENSE. Focus on the tension . . . (total of seven seconds after TENSE) and RELAX. Once again notice the difference in feeling between tension and relaxation. Feel the pleasant sensations as the muscles loosen and relax . . . (total of forty-five to sixty seconds after RELAX). Now focus on the muscles of your left hand and forearm . . . (In the interest of conserving space we will not include a complete transcript of relaxation instructions for all fourteen muscle groups. For each of the remaining twelve areas simply repeat the instructions for the upper right arm and substitute the appropriate anatomical name. Remember to use two tension-release cycles for each muscle group.)

At the end of the last tension-release phase: Now mentally explore each of the regions that you have relaxed. If you locate any remaining tension, then once again tense and relax any muscles in which tension remains. If you are now free from tension, just quietly savor the feelings of calmness and relaxation. (END OF INSTRUCTIONS)

Once your skeletal muscles are completely relaxed you will likely experience a profound inner sense of relaxation. If you wish to relax even more fully, we suggest the addition of a calm scene. The use of a calm scene involves visualizing some place where you feel (1) protected from the worries of this world, and (2) at peace with yourself. It can be any place that satisfies or nearly satisfies these requirements. Common choices are the seashore, the mountains, or one's own bed. After you have formed a mental picture of the place, project yourself into the scene. The idea is to do this in such a way that you actually feel that you are in the scene and not simply watching a movie of yourself in the scene. Whether or not you use the calm scene, allow yourself about five to ten minutes after the last tension-release cycle to enjoy the state you have achieved.

To gain maximum benefits from progressive relaxation you should practice it once (preferably twice) a day for several weeks. Relaxation is a skill. As with all skills, learning it requires practice. The regular practice of relaxation will make it an effective tool to use when you are under stress. Practice of the basic exercise is also necessary in preparing you to learn two shortcut methods, relaxation through recall and conditioned relaxation.

Relaxation through recall is a method of producing relaxation in the muscles without employing tension-release cycles. After you have practiced relaxation for several weeks and find that you can reliably produce a deep state of relaxation, you are ready to begin practicing relaxation through recall. This method depends on your ability (1) to recognize tension within your muscles and (2) to remember what it feels like to release tension from your muscles. Throughout training you have received instructions to focus all attention on the sensations associated with tension, tension release, and relaxation. Focusing on inner sensations during training will give you both the sensitivity to tension and the memory of how it feels to release tension that are necessary to this new skill. To use relaxation through recall you focus sequentially on each of the fourteen muscle groups, examining each for tension. If you find any tension present, then, while continuing to focus on that muscle group, recall what it felt like when you let go of tension in that area. The muscles will then relax. Proceed through each muscle group in this fashion.

Conditioned relaxation relies on forming a Pavlovian association between the feeling of relaxation and some cue word. The procedure is simple. Each time you practice relaxation, after you have become fully relaxed, direct all of your attention to your breathing. Each time you exhale say the word *relax* to yourself. Repeat this for thirty exhalations. You should practice this entire procedure at least once a week for four to five weeks. The regular and frequent pairing of the word *relax* with feelings of deep relaxation will invest the word itself with the power to lower your level of arousal. Once the association is formed, you can relax yourself at any time by closing your eyes, taking a deep breath, and saying the word *relax* to yourself.

Although the learning of relaxation requires much time and a special setting, relaxation is a practical and adaptable method for reducing arousal in real-life settings. During your initial efforts in learning relaxation it will require about thirty minutes to achieve deep relaxation. This time will be shortened considerably by a little practice. Trainees often find that after several sessions they are able to produce profound relaxation with only one tension-release cycle per muscle group. This cuts the time required in half. Learning relaxation through recall or conditioned relaxation can shorten the procedure still further. After one has learned to produce muscle relaxation in the optimal setting described earlier, one can learn to relax in everyday settings. Even when sitting in chairs that do not provide total support (or standing or walking), muscles that are not required for postural support can be relaxed. Taking relaxation breaks during times of acute stress or when chronic stress starts to mount is a basic part of the effective management of stress.

12

self-hypnosis
and
autosuggestion

Of the several stress reduction techniques discussed in this book, none is so thoroughly surrounded by misconception as hypnosis. For most people hypnosis conjures up a number of rather sensational stereotypes: the stage hypnotist with his bag of theatrical tricks; brainwashing and mind control of the sort represented in the film *The Manchurian Candidate*; or the psychoanalyst probing the deepest reaches of her patient's unconscious. The trouble with these stereotypes is that they represent only a small, rather melodramatic fraction of the various contexts in which hypnosis is applied. So prevalent are the many misconceptions circulating about hypnosis that it is probably wise to dispel some of the more common errors immediately, before going on to explain the relevance of hypnosis to the management of stress.

First of all, hypnosis is not sleep. It is analogous to sleep in virtually no important way. Hypnosis is, in fact, the antithesis of sleep in most respects. The hypnotic subject is not unconscious or unaware. Far from it—one who has entered an hypnotic state finds that his awareness and sensitivity have increased. The full range of mental faculties is available to one who is hypnotized.

Second, when one is hypnotized he does not surrender his will or lose control of himself. The image of a stiff-legged zombie created by the magic of hypnosis and under the control of the hypnotist has reality only in the minds of Hollywood scriptwriters. It is only the conscious sensation of control that is altered during hypnosis. Losing the feeling that one is consciously and actively regulating one's actions may be threatening to those who have the need to run a tight psychological ship, but this fear is without basis. Entering the state of hypnosis is analogous to a pilot's taking his hands from the wheel, putting his airplane on automatic pilot, and sitting back for a brief rest. The pilot is available for any emergency. He has not parachuted from the aircraft.

Third, the hypnotic state is not a spell or trance that results from the skill or power of a hypnotist who projects this trance onto a subject. Nothing could be further from the truth. The ability to enter the hypnotic state is one that we all possess to a greater or lesser degree. When we enter this state either through the efforts of a hypnotist or through self-hypnosis, the same fundamental process occurs. Most of us frequently slip in and out of the hypnotic state spontaneously without the assistance of a hypnotist or auto-hypnotic procedures. So in learning self-hypnosis you will not be developing an ability that you do not already have. Rather you will be learning some methods for systematically and more effectively tapping an ability that you currently possess.

You may be asking yourself what hypnosis is if it has been misrepresented in the popular media. Hypnosis can be defined very simply: Hypnosis is the altered state of consciousness that results from focusing awareness on a set of suggestions and allowing oneself to be receptive to those suggestions—all while allowing free rein to one's powers of imagination. The depth or intensity of the hypnotic state can vary greatly. In a light trance individuals show physical and mental relaxation as well as the ability to respond to simple suggestions. In a medium trance subjects can become numb to pain and forget what has happened during hypnosis. In deep trance the subject can experience recall of lost memories and experience visual hallucinations. What follows are some suggestions typical of those used in hypnotic inductions.

Sit back. Find a comfortable posture and let yourself relax. Now focus your attention on your arms. Imagine that your arms are getting heavy, very heavy. Feel them pressing down into the armrests of the chair. Let the heaviness increase so that with each passing moment the weight of your arms increases. Now imagine that your arms have become so heavy that you cannot raise them, no matter how hard you try.

The basic features of hypnotic induction are well illustrated by these instructions. Had you responded to these suggestions by entering a light hypnotic trance, the following processes would have occurred:

1. You would have become comfortable and relaxed.
2. You would have concentrated your awareness on instructions suggesting some change in your sensations or in the way you were perceiving the world.
3. You would have allowed yourself to respond to those suggestions.
4. You would have used your imagination to allow yourself to actually feel the change in sensation.
5. You would have temporarily put aside some measure of the active, self-conscious control you normally exercise over your thoughts and behavior.

Does this sound too easy? If the process we have described sounds too pat, too simple and straightforward to account for the magic you associate with hypnosis, this may mean that you are still confusing the reality of hypnosis with one of its popular stereotypes. Remember also that we are not suggesting that you can learn quickly and without expert help to explore all of the many fascinating possibilities that have been achieved through hypnosis. Our goal is to teach you how to achieve the minimal alteration of consciousness that is sufficient to facilitate relaxation and autosuggestion. We are interested in stress reduction, not in age regression, exploration of the unconscious, or the production of bodily anesthesia. These latter phenomena require the medium-to-deep trance that is best sought with the assistance of a skilled hypnotist.

As we employ it, hypnosis can be used as part of a stress reduction program in two ways. First, hypnosis can be an excellent method of relaxation. Research has shown that hypnotic instructions are very effective in producing lowered physiological arousal and feelings of inner calm. Much as in the fashion of progressive relaxation and meditation, one can, under hypnosis, elicit the relaxation response described in earlier chapters. It is possible while hypnotized to give yourself suggestions that are effective in lessening tension and anxiety.

Second, hypnosis can be used to change your thinking and behavior in ways that will reduce the stress you experience. While hypnotized you can reaffirm and reinforce a commitment to change both beliefs and behavior. When you are hypnotized you are more receptive to suggestions you wish to follow. Thus it is possible to use the hypnotic state as an opportunity to reprogram your mental computer in desired directions.

What, then, must you do in order to begin using self-hypnosis as a tool in your efforts to reduce stress? For one to effectively utilize self-hypnosis four factors seem to be important:

1. *An open and receptive mind.* Excessive skepticism, fear, or distrust makes it almost impossible for one to be hypnotized. To be hypnotized you must go with the suggestions. A show-me attitude makes entering the hypnotic state quite laborious and difficult. In these few pages we cannot possibly prove to you that self-hypnosis will be useful. All we ask is that you attempt it with an open mind.

2. *Motivation.* As is the case with attempting anything new or unusual, it is important that one strongly desire to learn.

3. *Time and a peaceful setting.* Distractions make learning self-hypnosis extraordinarily difficult. We suggest you choose surroundings similar to those outlined in the chapter on meditation.

4. *An effective set of hypnotic suggestions.*

Before you attempt self-hypnosis, there are some general guidelines that should be followed. It is important not to strain or try hard to become hypnotized. Too much active effort is a hindrance rather than a help. During your initial attempts, don't ask yourself the question "Am I really hypnotized?" If you are feeling relaxed and calm you have probably entered at least a very light trance. There are methods for determining the depth of trance, but these are beyond the scope of this book. If you wish to accurately gauge the depth of your hypnotic forays, we suggest that you consult a professional hypnotist. For our aims it is only necessary that you achieve a state of consciousness in which you feel relaxed and receptive, while at the same time being able to concentrate your attention on suggestions. Keep in mind that you will be aware and in control at all times.

What follows are two sets of instructions for inducing self-hypnosis. The first is the eye fixation method, which is probably the most widely used of all self-hypnosis techniques. The second is an adaptation of the method perfected by Dr. Herbert Spiegel of Columbia University. We have used both methods with excellent results. Before embarking on your course of self-hypnosis, be certain to read this entire chapter. Then reread several times the instructions for the method of induction that you have chosen to employ first.

For the eye fixation method assume a comfortable position and find some stationary object to fix your attention upon. This object could be anything. Often used are a candle flame or a spot on the wall or ceiling positioned just above eye level, one that produces some tension in the eye muscles when you stare at it. Silently tell yourself that as you look at the object your eyelids will begin to feel heavier and heavier—that shortly they will be so heavy that you cannot keep them open. Say to yourself that when they close you will enter a state of relaxation and full awareness. Repeat this suggestion to yourself every sixty seconds. Focus your attention on your eyelids. Concentrate on their increasing heaviness. When you are ready, allow them to close. When your eyes have closed, slowly take a deep breath and hold it for about ten or fifteen seconds. Then gradually let the air out and, as your lungs and chest relax, let that relaxation spread all over your body. Let your breathing become slow and comfortable. Whenever you exhale say the word *relax* to yourself. Imagine that each time you exhale, you are breathing out of your body any remaining tension and anxiety. After a few minutes of this slow, regular breathing, you should feel relaxed and comfortable.

An alternative to the eye fixation technique is the eye roll induction. As with the eye fixation method you begin by assuming a comfortable posture. Look straight ahead. Without moving your head, roll your eyes upward so that your gaze is tilted toward an imaginary spot at the center top of your forehead. Without changing the position of your eyes, close your eyes. Simultaneously with the closing of your eyes take a deep breath and hold it. Then, at the same time, let out the breath and let your eyes return to their normal position and relax. As you exhale imagine that your body is becoming very heavy. Focus on the feeling of heaviness as it increases and the sensation of your body pressing down into the chair. One by one concentrate on each major muscle group of your body. Start with your forearms. Tell yourself that your forearms are beginning to feel warm and that they are feeling still heavier. Let the warmth and heaviness in your arms increase until you feel that it would require a supreme effort to try to move your forearms. Then shift attention to your upper arms. Repeat this process for these muscles and for the following muscle groups: facial muscles, neck and shoulders, chest, back muscles, abdomen, buttocks, thighs, and calves. When you have completed this process you will feel calm and peaceful.

After completing the first phase of induction using either the eye fixation or eye roll method, you are ready to deepen your trance. Begin by taking another deep breath. Hold it for about ten seconds. Slowly exhale and, as you do, say the word *deeper* to yourself several times. Say to yourself, "Now I am going still deeper." Picture yourself at the top of a slow-moving escalator that is going down. See yourself step onto the escalator. As you ride the escalator downward say the word *deeper* to yourself and feel yourself letting go—allowing yourself to sink into trance. When you reach the bottom, step off the escalator and visualize yourself walking slowly to another escalator that will take you downward to the next level. Step onto it and repeat the entire process. In all you should continue to ride until you have achieved the level of trance that feels comfortable and appropriate to you. Remember you are always in control of how deep you go. Actually, it doesn't matter whether you ride an escalator, or an elevator, or walk down a flight of stairs. You might experiment with all three images, eventually settling upon the one that seems to best produce the desired effect of helping you imagine that you are going deeper.

Another deepening exercise that you may use in addition to or as an alternative to the escalator image is to imagine yourself in front of a blackboard with a piece of chalk in your right hand and a blackboard eraser in your left hand. Visualize yourself writing the number 10 on the blackboard. Look at it for a second and then slowly erase it. As you erase the number say the word *deeper* to yourself. Count backward one at a time. Continue to write and erase numbers until you have erased the number 1. Using either or both of these deepening techniques you should be able to increase the sensations of comfort and relaxation that were achieved after the first phase of induction.

When deepening your trance there are some guidelines that should be followed:

1. Never go deeper than you wish to go. A very light trance is all that you need achieve. Because you can bring yourself out of trance at any time you wish, there is no danger in going as deep as you wish to go.
2. Never give yourself a suggestion that makes you uncomfortable. This will simply make you tense and prevent you from achieving the level of trance that you desire. For example, if you feel uncomfortable in making your body heavy, make it light. If you don't like to go down, go up instead. The important thing is that you give yourself suggestions that involve some shift of your present state of awareness.

Keep in mind that while you are hypnotized you will be aware and in control at all times. To exit from the state, all you ever need do is to tell yourself the following: "I wish to come out of trance. As I count from one to five my eyelids will open. At two there will be movement sensations in my eyelids. At three my eyelids will begin to flutter. At four my eyes will be partially open. At five my eyes will be wide open and I will no longer be in trance. I will feel refreshed and relaxed." (Then count) One . . . Two . . . Three . . . Four . . . Five. Most people prefer to come out of trance gradually. If you prefer a speedier exit, you can simply say "I'm coming out," and open your eyes.

Once you have achieved a light trance you are ready to give yourself suggestions that will assist you in reducing stress. Our description of hypnotic induction shows that much of the procedure involves suggestions of relaxation. So by the end of the deepening phase you should already be very relaxed. If, however, you feel any residual tension at this point you may suggest to yourself that you will relax more deeply each time you exhale. Tell yourself that you will continue to relax until you are as comfortable as you wish to be. Used in this way, self-hypnosis is analogous to meditation and progressive relaxation. It can be a simple, straightforward way of bringing you relief from tension and preventing arousal from building to uncomfortable levels.

Self-hypnosis, however, potentially offers more than an alternative means to relaxation. This is due to the mechanism of posthypnotic suggestions. These are suggestions whose effects extend beyond the hypnotic session, which influence behavior and thinking after one is no longer in trance.

Posthypnotic suggestions can be of value in two ways: (1) They can reinforce a commitment to behave or think differently; (2) They can be a force in creating a commitment to reorient one's life. In either mode, autosuggestion facilitates changes people wish to make in their lives. You may have read of the use of hypnosis in overcoming problems of overweight, cigarette smoking, and insomnia. Self-hypnosis can be a powerful tool in any kind of self-change effort. This is because through the use of autosuggestion we are able to present ourselves with desirable propaganda at the time when we are most susceptible to be influenced.

In principle, you can give yourself any kind of suggestion while hypnotized. You can tell yourself general things such as that in each day that follows you will see fewer events as awful and catastrophic. Or you may give yourself very specific suggestions such as "Getting angry at my wife when she infrequently chooses not to have sex with me only poisons and damages me. She is entitled to the pursuit of her own happiness and to make her own decisions."

One of the best sources for helpful suggestions are the guidelines in Chapter 7 on cognitive change methods for developing calming beliefs and positive self-talk. Self-hypnosis and autosuggestion methods can be an effective aid to weaving more rational and relaxing perspectives into the fabric of everyday life.

There are some principles of suggestion that should be followed if your suggestions are to be maximally effective.

1. *Repetition:* The more you repeat a suggestion the more effective it will be. All advertising operates on this principle.

2. *Positiveness:* Phrase your suggestions positively. Avoid negatives. Instead of telling yourself that you shouldn't, mustn't, won't, or can't be in a hurry, tell yourself that starting tomorrow you will begin to feel more relaxed and slowed down when faced with deadlines or appointments.

3. *Gradualism:* Don't set yourself up for failure by telling yourself something like "When I come out of trance I will be free from tension forever." Hypnosis is a tool that can aid you in developing the skills of coping with stress; it is not magic. Tell yourself that as each day goes by you will feel more relaxed and that your commitment to perceive the world as unstressful will grow stronger and be easier to carry out.

4. *Results:* Keep your suggestions couched in the language of special actions rather than general intentions. Don't say you'll try not to seek the approval of everyone. To "try" at something implies that failure may be likely. This kind of construction lessens the power of a suggestion. Tell yourself instead that you can begin to feel an increasing sense of self-confidence, even when people disapprove of you.

5. *Orders:* It is best not to phrase a suggestion so that it sounds like an order. Few of us fail to resist, at some level, when we are ordered to do something. This is true even of commands we give ourselves. For example, in-

stead of "I must" or "I have to," use "I choose to" or "I can."

6. *Images:* Whenever you can combine an appropriate visual image with a verbal suggestion, it makes the suggestion more powerful. For example, if you are giving yourself a suggestion to slow down, it would be helpful to simultaneously picture yourself walking slowly to an important meeting or calmly driving within the speed limit, even though you are late for an appointment. Imagery is very important. Use it whenever you can. For many readers it will be a more potent agent of suggestion and change than verbal statements.

If you follow these rules, you will improve your chances of effectively using autosuggestion in your life.

13

conclusion

We have considered a variety of approaches to reducing stress in everyday living. Some of these techniques emphasize rethinking deep-seated attitudes and beliefs. Other approaches focus on changing one's outward behavior or altering one's environment to make it more conducive to a low-stress life style. Still other methods involve learning to lower physiological arousal directly. It is our aim in this chapter to give some general guidelines for the use of our techniques and to provide a practical discussion of the enterprise of self-change.

Most self-help books are failures. They bring lasting benefit only to those who collect royalties from them. After an initial reading of these books, people usually feel a sense of optimism and exhilaration. Believing that their lives can be bettered, they often make some initial positive changes. Six months later, however, it is as though the book had never been read. We want you to avoid that fate. The recommendations which follow will enable you to make optimal use of the stress reduction methods in this book and will increase your chances for lasting success in your efforts to cope with stress.

1. *Don't try to transform yourself overnight.* Avoid the trap of trying to battle stress on all fronts simultaneously. You can try, but you will not succeed. Too many self-change efforts in too many directions in themselves can create tension and frustration. Unrealistic expectations and overwork can insidiously creep into your efforts to become a more relaxed individual. Pick out one or two of our techniques and begin applying them to one or two specific areas of your life. Don't overdo it.

2. *Walk before you run.* Take small steps. Don't tackle your biggest, most difficult stress problems first. Attempt to deal with those situations which are most likely to bring you early success. Don't kid yourself. You will be more likely to continue your efforts to cope constructively if your first attempts are, at least, partially successful. Structure your initial efforts so as to help yourself slowly build the confidence and skills you need to attack the really difficult problems.

3. *Don't expect to "cure" yourself.* Expect setbacks. Stress is an inescapable part of life. You can never entirely evade it. Some of your newly acquired coping skills will let you down at a time when you need them most. Even when you believe you have completely changed an old pattern of thought, you will occasionally return to that old way of thinking when the going gets rough. Any change, especially basic belief change, is a taxing and repetitive process. Often the same ground must be gone over many times. But remember, the goal is improvement, not perfection. Focus on your overall pattern of improvement, not on individual setbacks.

4. *Keep your self-worth out of it.* As is the case with any undertaking, your efforts toward stress reduction can be the target of self-evaluation. In your efforts at self-improvement, don't erect still another standard to measure yourself against. Don't focus on how well or how quickly you are lessening stress. Focus instead on enjoying and learning from the process of change. Remember,

your goal is to reduce stress, not to become the best stress reducer on the block.

5. *Expect change to be compartmentalized.* When you learn how to lower stress in one area of your life, don't expect that other life areas will improve automatically. For example, learning to dissipate anger experienced at home may do very little to lower one's hostility at work. Although any positive change will likely make us feel better about ourselves and give us added confidence that change is possible, most stress-producing situations have to be tackled individually.

6. *Enlist the aid of others.* Tell those who care about you that you are making efforts to change. Share your goals with them. Once informed, others can be valuable sources of information, encouragement and support. Furthermore, efforts toward self-change (even positive self-change) can be confusing and upsetting to our friends and loved ones. If they know what you are attempting, your changed behavior will be more comhensible to them and less disruptive to your relationships.

7. *Keep some kind of diary or journal.* In Chapter 7 we describe one useful kind of diary. A diary not only gives you a record of your progress, but also helps you to focus your efforts toward stress reduction. Keeping a daily journal requires very little time but makes you a much more accurate observer on the situations you face and your reactions to them. This increased awareness can trigger both insights and changes. It is sometimes essential to discovering the beliefs and patterns of coping that are involved in your experience of stress.

8. *Learn one of the relaxation methods.* Sample all three. Pick the one that seems to work best for you, then learn it well. The ability to relax yourself at will without ingesting drugs is an invaluable part of any stress reduction program.

The preceding guidelines can, if followed, greatly enhance the effectiveness of your stress reduction program. So too can a certain perspective on life and living.

We must remember each day the nature of our existential

predicament. Despite our capacities for self-delusion and for "losing ourselves" in our work, our fantasies, or our problems, we can hide only temporarily from one fact. At every moment our time is running out. Each of us, as Yeats said, is "fastened to a dying animal." Life is finite.

Hiding from our mortality is seldom effective, wastes a great deal of energy, and is ultimately destructive. On the other hand, living with a daily awareness of the brevity and finitude of life can help us clarify our values, find direction and meaning, and waste as little time as possible. In relation to eternity, each of us is granted such a tiny fragment of existence. We hope you make the most of your life.

suggested readings

Carrington, Patricia. *Freedom in Meditation*. Garden City, New York: Doubleday, 1977.

Deutsch, Morton. *The Resolution of Conflict*. New Haven: Yale University Press, 1973.

Ellis, Albert and Harper, Robert A. *A New Guide to Rational Living*. Englewood Cliffs, New Jersey: Prentice-Hall, 1975.

Friedman, Meyer and Rosenman, Ray H. *Type A Behavior and Your Heart,* New York: Knopf, 1974.

Lakein, Alan. *How to Get Control of Your Time and Your Life.* New York: Peter Wyden, 1973.

Lazarus, Arnold A. *Behavior Therapy and Beyond*. New York: McGraw-Hill, 1971.

Lazarus, Richard S. *Psychological Stress and the Coping Process*. New York: McGraw-Hill, 1966.

Meichenbaum, Donald H. *Cognitive Behavior Modification.* New York: Plenum, 1977.

index

Recommended Reading from SIGNET and MENTOR

SIGNET and MENTOR Books of Special Interest

☐ **PSYCHOPATHOLOGY OF EVERYDAY LIFE by Sigmund Freud.** The celebrated analyst's easily understood explanation of the hidden causes of everyday errors.
(#ME1656—$1.75)†

☐ **TEST YOUR OWN MENTAL HEALTH by William Gladstone.** An exciting new test of over 100 insightful questions that will, in less than an hour, give you a "pictograph" of the intricate goings-on in your mind. By checking off symptoms in seven categories, you can now determine whether you fit the norm, whether you're a neurotic coper, or whether you require professional help. (#E8757—$1.95)*

☐ **WINNERS & LOSERS: The Art of Self-Image Modification by Dr. Howard M. Newburger and Marjorie Lee.** How to play the game of life—to win! Are you getting less out of life than you'd like? Would you like to break your loser habits and make yourself a winner? Here is a psychologist's dramatic new way of showing you how you can do this by yourself, swiftly and effectively, without costly therapy.
(#W6504—$1.50)

☐ **BT—BEHAVIOR THERAPY: Strategies for Solving Problems in Living by Spencer A. Rathus, Ph.D., and Jeffrey S. Nevid, Ph.D.** Take charge of #1—with today's most effective method of self-help and self-improvement.
(#E8085—$2.25)

☐ **NEW PATHWAYS IN PSYCHOLOGY: Maslow and the Post-Freudian Revolution by Colin Wilson.** The life and work of the pioneering American psychologist who explored the limits of man's higher consciousness. (#MJ1315—$1.95)†

* Price slightly higher in Canada
† Not available in Canada

To order these titles, please

use coupon on next page.